Safe in the Perimeter

of His Hands

The True Account of a Young Soldier in Vietnam

By
Thomas North and Daisy Willard

Summerland Publishing
Offices in Salt Lake City, UT and Summerland, CA
www.summerlandpublishing.com
Email: summerlandpublishing@gmail.com

Printed in the United States of America.

ISBN #: 978-1-7375730-6-7

Library of Congress # 2022903431

Dedication

This book is dedicated to the men I fought alongside of and to those who didn't make it home.

It's dedicated to my God, who I know is standing beside me and often carrying me.

Finally, its dedicated to my wife, Jennifer. You mean the world to me! Thank you for making a family with me, for being my partner through this life, for listening. I don't always show it and sometimes I don't say it, but I love you and all that you have brought to my life.

Acknowledgment

This book would not have been possible without the constant support from Jennifer North, Tim Willard, Emma Tabaldo and Noah Tabaldo. Thank you for being there through all the rough drafts, tears and moments of doubt. We love you!

Thank you to Alicia, Allison and Antoinette for your editing inputs.

Finally, thank you Jolinda for walking me through this process. I hope this is the first of many books!

Table of Contents

Forward

By Daisy Willard

This book has nothing to do with political views or the debate between war and peace. This book is about a soldier, a young man, who received the call from his country, and he answered it. Thomas North, my father.

I am so very honored to be a part of this production, to have shared in the compiling of these memories for generations to come.

This project has been a serious part of my life for over fifteen years. My first memory of Dad's war experience was at a very young age. He was sitting in our green rocking chair asleep, and I went to wake him by placing a hand on his arm and calling his name. One second, I was beside him and the next I was knocked into the walk-in closet that was inches from the chair. I had startled him, but lesson learned – call out to him, don't touch him. It was just one aspect of the war still holding onto him. I've seen him go from a standing position to the floor when a loud sound goes off; those reflexes, honed so many years ago, still embedded.

When Dad and I first started working on his stories, it wasn't even with the thought of putting it into a book, it was a dad and daughter, often sitting in the hot tub, just talking. We would talk about life and end up with Vietnam. The more I heard, the more I wanted to hear, and the more he wanted to share.

Dad confided in me recently that when he was evaluated at the

VA Hospital and asked about his PTSD, he stated that talking with me about it has helped the most. I feel that this book has bonded us closer than anything else and has helped him work through some of that PTSD.

It is with great love and respect I present my father's story. He has always been my hero, the man I look up to. He has taught me so much. I cherish all our memories, those of camping, sitting in Bible studies and just talking.

I love you Dad!

Our Heroes

Among the laughter, the sneers and spitting,

these men walked proudly.

They had been drafted, they had fought with courage,

they had survived.

No one was waving them home, no welcoming speeches,

no words of praise.

These men were our heroes of Nam.

Today they still stand strong, just as they did that day, walking off the

plane that brought them to their homeland, the Freeland.

These men are our patriots of freedom, our crusaders of justice, our

champions of democracy.

These are our heroes.

Written by

Daisy M. North (Willard)

2003

Chapter One — The Calling

With the mortars falling and the artillery firing, the soldier thinks only for the moment. Instinct kicks in and with adrenaline rushing, no one questions why the soldier standing next to you falls and you remain; I didn't until I came to Christ and then my whole outlook changed. I am here for a purpose.

"The Lord will work out his plans for my life – for your faithful love, O Lord, endures forever. Don't abandon me, for you made me."

Psalm 138:8

It was the spring of 1967, with love and peace the sign of the times. The 'love movement' was going strong with San Francisco becoming congested, President Lyndon Johnson was in office, and I received a draft notice into the United States Army. I was only twenty years old and remember thinking, 'I'm old enough to die for my country but too young to vote or drink.'

The continued presence of American troops in Vietnam totaled a staggering 475,000 with the peace rallies at home multiplying. Martin Luther King Jr. was speaking out against the war and protesters were increasing by the thousands.

I reported to Portland, Oregon, for a physical and official swearing in on July 12th, 1967. Protesters were gathered outside the area of induction, waving signs and demanding an end to the war and draftees were escaping to Canada to avoid it.

Before Congress made improvements to the draft in 1971, a man could qualify for a student deferment if he was able to show full-time enrollment and making satisfactory progress toward a degree. College attendance increased eight percent from 1963 to 1968 and plummeted between 1968 and 1973. I didn't try to leave, and I didn't join a college. I definitely didn't want to go to war, but my country called me and I answered.

Each inductee had to take an aptitude test before they could be placed into a military occupational specialty or MOS. The better you did on the test, the more options you had to choose from. They placed the test in front of me and I didn't even read it but instead just marked down answers, honestly not caring where I was placed. The ones in charge weren't quite as naive as I thought. I was sent to Fort Lewis, Washington for nine weeks of basic training and I had to retake the test, this time reading it.

The Army career counselor met with me after and suggested some options: Stay in four years and be a helicopter mechanic or eight years and be a pilot. I looked him square in the eye and said, "you've got me for two." I was assigned the MOS of light weapons infantryman.

Fort Lewis

When they printed my dog tags, I was asked what religion I wanted on it, and I responded that I had no religion and "no preference" was listed. The drill sergeant, a big tough guy, told me to get a religion because more than likely I would end up in Vietnam.

3

While at Fort Lewis, there was an outbreak of spinal meningitis and all the companies trained alone. We were told it wasn't how things were usually done, but we were under a strict quarantine and didn't see any other companies. It was during this time that I was volunteered to give blood since I was type O.

Basic training was just that; they taught you the basics. How to shave, iron your clothes, clean your shoes, personal hygiene, army rules and regulations, and how to march and fire weapons.

It was at Fort Lewis where I qualified with the M-14, a fully automatic .30 caliber rifle and earned the expert marksmanship qualification badge with rifle bar.

I never had any problem with the training or the weapons. I was physically fit, having done track, cross country, and wrestling in high school. For the past two years I'd worked side by side with WWII veterans at a sawmill and held my own with them physically and verbally. These men were rough and tough with language to prove it.

I went to work at the mill in May of 1965 and was allowed time off to graduate in June. The two-story mill had a lunchroom by the pond that was reached by a thirty-foot catwalk. One day I was headed to the lunchroom when a guy ran up behind me, after bragging to the crew he was going to 'push the kid into the pond'. I did a wrestling maneuver and had him face down in a matter of seconds. He was older than me and made a fool of himself that day in front of the older men. I made lifelong friends that day including Jim Fry who was 38 at that time and just passed away at the age of 91. He was a good man, a mentor.

Our days at Fort Lewis started with reveille at 0530 and formations at 0600 and then the daily dozen; a dozen different exercises and a one-mile run. I could easily keep up with the leaders, but I remember some of the other guys struggled with this.

In September, I was sent to Fort Polk, Louisiana — nicknamed Tiger Land — for nine weeks of jungle training where I did advanced infantry training. During this time, I experienced my first taste of segregation. Having grown up in the Northwest, I just hadn't been around very many African Americans and I quickly learned it was all different in the south.

While at a bus depot, I climbed into a taxicab heading to the airport. The driver, a very nice black man, turned around and said,

"Son, you're in the wrong cab." It was there, in Leesville, that I also saw the water fountains labeled 'black' and 'white'.

Fort Polk was the only combat training center that also trained and deployed combat units. I was amazed through these nine weeks that guys were being kicked out of the infantry and put into armored personal. I honestly thought that anyone could be infantry, that they put the dumb guys there. I discovered that those of us remaining were a uniformed group of guys appearing to be close in height and weight and that infantry really was a skill, a science.

Fort Polk had a small portion filled with dense, jungle-like vegetation and it was always hot and humid — like Vietnam's muggy weather — in theory it would acclimatize new soldiers for Vietnam combat.

Those nine weeks of training consisted of becoming familiar and proficient in firing the .45 caliber pistol, which I qualified on. The M-79, a single shot, shoulder-fired, break action grenade launcher and the M-60 machine gun, which I earned an expert marksmanship qualification badge with a machine gun bar. We also trained on the M16, where I earned the sharpshooter marksmanship qualification badge with rifle bar.

The M-16 used fiberglass instead of wood on the stock and hand guards. It was comprised of aluminum instead of steel, making it shorter and lighter than the previous M-14. The ammo was also smaller and lighter making it easier to carry more.

Week five was bivouac, which I discovered was a military term for camping without shelter or protection from enemy fire. We learned to make tents by combining two ponchos and were instructed on how to dig a foxhole according to army regulations. I didn't find the thought of camping out a problem, I had been camping most of my youth.

When I was thirteen, a few friends and I grabbed our fishing poles, sleeping bags and packs to walk across the hills, about 20 miles, to some falls. We would camp for ten days, swimming and living off the fish we caught; we did this most summers.

Week six the army fired live rounds at targets as we walked and crawled through various obstacles and training courses. One obstacle was actually kind of fun; there was a rope on a pully, and you had to drop into the water before you collided with the bank on the opposite side.

Most days were spent on our belly, cradling our weapon in our arms out in front of us and moving along using elbows and knees to propel us forward. After that we were trained on evasive tactics and ways to avoid being captured. This included map reading and compass use, which I excelled at. We also learned about calling in a Sit Rep, Situation Report. This would be called in every hour. If there was no activity you would just say 'Sit Rep Negative,' however if there was activity it became positive, and you would explain what was happening. The goal was to keep communication short and to the point.

There was a field of 100 meters and each person had to learn their pace to measure it. They said it was important to have something to keep track of your counting, like small stones, and move them from one pocket to another. So, for each 100 meters walked, a stone would be moved. I didn't have to use this method, I was just able to keep track, but I know others did.

Pacing was practiced in any down time we had because it was vital that we could get to an area and call-in marker rounds, the first round fired by mortars or artillery. The marker round was then used to adjust the following rounds onto the target.

In week eight, they told us about the edible vegetation in case we were detached from our platoon. I remember being outside for this instruction, we were standing around listening to the instructor when a cottonmouth snake crawled out of the underbrush. The instructor used that opportunity to present another meal option if we were on our own. We killed the snake and then boiled it in a canteen cup. Let me tell you, it does not taste like chicken!

One of the final trainings was to transport us to an outlying area and drop us. We had two instructions: get back and don't get caught by the 'enemy'. I saw the 'enemy' twice, but they walked right past me. I remember just easing behind a tree and walking around it the opposite way. I made it back to camp without a problem. If you were spotted, then they took you to a holding place and tortured you. It consisted of being put in a 55-gallon drum that had water in it. They dropped you in and put the lid on.

When the training finally came to an end, I had a twenty-two day leave before I was deployed to Vietnam. I traveled back to Oregon and visited with parents and five siblings until my time to leave country.

As I boarded the Braniff airline, a very luxurious craft, in Oakland, California for the twenty-seven-hour flight to Vietnam, I felt anxious and a bit nervous. I was seated next to an E5 buck sergeant in his early twenties. For the story's sake, we will call him Hank. He had spent two to three years in Germany and made his rank there. His MOS was infantry. He talked about how he had been trying to get transfer orders to Vietnam because, as he put it, "I'm a trained killer and I want to put it to use."

I didn't say much to him about that. Although I'd been through jungle training at Fort Polk, I honestly didn't feel I was a trained killer. I just hoped I was trained enough to be a survivor. I had wrestled four years in high school and found that the cocky ones who were so sure they would win, often were the losers.

I think if I had known the Lord at this point, I would have sent a prayer up. But looking back, God knew who I was and already had angels assigned to me.

The plane landed in the Philippines for refueling and everyone had to disembark. They said it would take a couple hours, and I took the opportunity to use the bathroom facilities. It was a dark room with a row of toilets. They didn't have any tanks on them, just the commode seat. After doing my business I looked for a handle to flush but didn't see any. Thinking this was odd, I walked over to a small sink to wash my hands when, out of the corner of my eye, I saw movement.

An old woman got up from a squatting position, picked up a bucket and carried it over to the toilet I had just vacated and poured the water in, thereby flushing it. I hadn't even seen her in that corner. It was quite a wakeup call: I wasn't in the US of A anymore!

Aerial view of a Village

When the doors opened at Bien Hoa, Vietnam, the heat and humidity slapped me full in the face. The air, thick with smoke from the burning latrines, made my eyes tear up; the humidity and burnt waste smell making me gag.

On our left was a line of soldiers; they looked considerably older than us. Maybe it was the tan they all had or the constant lack of sleep, I later realized most lived with, but as I marched past and looked them in the eyes, there was an age not measurable in years but in experience.

The horrors those innocent boys had witnessed and been a part of had changed them for life. The person who had landed in this war-torn country was gone and in his place was a man; a man his family wouldn't recognize, and society wouldn't know what to do with; we looked like kids in comparison to them.

I was held for a day or two in Bien Hoa, having been sent to Vietnam as a 'replacement,' until the army could assign me to a unit. Shortly after arriving I was told to report to the supply clerk, a SPC 4, and get my jungle fatigues.

Let me take a quick second to explain the military ranking system. An E1, what I was coming in as, was a private. E-2 was a private 2, E-3 was private first class, E-4 was a specialist (SPC) or a corporal (CPL), E-5 was a sergeant and E-6 was a staff sergeant. It continues through E-9, a sergeant major. This particular supply clerk was an E-4, so he outranked me.

I went into the supply depot and asked for my fatigues. The E-4 replied with, "Give me ten." I just stared at him, a little disbelieving I was being bullied and told to do ten pushups in order to acquire my clothes. I replied with, "What are you going to do if I don't, send me to

Vietnam?" He just smirked, I think appreciating my retort, and handed over the fatigues.

I was assigned to the 101st Airborne, the 1st of the 502 and quickly told them that it had to be a mistake; I hadn't been through jump school. I was told that it didn't matter, everything was done with helicopters these days.

The 101st 1st/502 landed in Vietnam on December 13th, 1967, and this was the last week of February 1968. They had so many casualties, that the companies were in desperate need of replacements. So off I went to five days of Preparation Training for my new home. This was also referred to as Screaming Eagle Replacement Training School.

This training was different from that at Fort Polk. This was 'life and death in Vietnam' training including booby traps and trip flares that were set up in a realistic village and jungle trail. There were classes in first aid and sanitation. Reaction courses were set during the day with guard duty at night preparing you for the time ahead when you wouldn't be able to sleep. The occasional unscheduled mortar attack confirmed the fact that you were now in the army.

Safe in the Perimeter of His Hands

One of the instructors told us that, 'In case of an explosion, tighten up your muscles as tight as you can so the shrapnel won't penetrate you'. Wow, I thought, if the airborne has people believing they are the Man of Steel, then I'm really on my own out here. While working in the sawmill, I saw a nine-foot ban saw come apart and it rained shrapnel throughout the mill. The building was supported by 12x12 timbers, and the shrapnel cut gauges into them big enough to take an arm off. I knew firsthand what flying pieces of metal could do; it could kill.

Within a couple of days after P-Training, I found myself with a handful of others being flown, trucked and finally arriving at Landing Zone Sally just north of Hue in the Quang Tri Province. It was said to have been named after one of the general's daughters.

Chapter Two — They're Trying to Kill Me

I arrived in the afternoon of March 25th. I was issued an M16 rifle with instructions to target practice at the garbage dump, and 'don't shoot any of the kids rummaging through it'. The M16 is a lightweight, semi and fully automatic magazine-fed assault rifle; you could walk the rounds right up someone and didn't have to be accurate.

We didn't go to bed that night, instead I loaded my ruck sack. It included combat rations (c-rations) for five days; these were canned meals for use in the field. Each usually consisted of a canned entree, a can of fruit, pack of dessert, a pack of powdered cocoa, a small pack of 4 cigarettes and 2 pieces of chewing gum.

I put in a basic load of ammo: six grenades, two blocks of c-4, a claymore mine and two trip flares. The claymore mine was used primarily as a perimeter defense weapon. When triggered, it would explode in a fan-shaped pattern and send pellets like a shotgun. I also had a can of machine gun ammo on my pack. After it was loaded, it weighed about a hundred pounds.

Safe in the Perimeter of His Hands

I went to a church service that evening, at the recommendation of the sergeant in charge. The priest handed out small metals to protect us in battle. It had the image of a woman, standing on the earth with a parachute around her. The words 'Our Lady Queen of Angels Defend us in Combat' surrounded the sides. I still didn't believe in anything higher, but I wasn't one to turn down good advice, so I went to the service and accepted the metal, keeping it on my dog tags throughout the duration of my stay in country.

At midnight the company, made up of 100 men, left on foot into the foothills of the jungle. There were three platoons of about thirty men, each platoon has three squads of ten guys. Then there was the headquarters group included the captain, a ranking sergeant, the Forward Observer, usually a lieutenant; all of them having their own Radio Telephone Operator.

I was in the front platoon in the second squad, so about in the middle with the captain in front. The first squad was guard to the headquarters group and the second squad was first back up followed by the third. I have to say this is the only time during my tour of duty that I saw the headquarters group in the front. After this, they were always towards the back and a point man was in front.

I wasn't told anything about the mission, as I was just a new guy. We walked all night through rice paddies and on the dikes between them. I remember the humidity being staggering, especially with my hundred-pound pack on. We waded through streams that varied in their depth from waist to chest and continued walking through foothills that were open, into the thick dense jungle.

Daylight was starting to break through the jungle when we made contact with the North Vietnamese Army. The North Vietnamese was the 'enemy' of the war, but they had allies in the South, which the US called Viet Cong but were officially known as the National Liberation Front of South Vietnam. They were a communist revolutionary organization that had both guerilla and regular army units. They were within the South, embedded within its people, its culture, its landscape. They made it impossible to know if a villager was innocent or just in disguise. They made it impossible to draw the line between good guys and bad. They made the war deadly.

One moment we were walking along, I was wet and tired and thinking I would like to be anywhere but here when suddenly blasts of rounds were going off over us. There was gun fire and explosions towards the front of the line. Everyone hit the ground, but it was apparent that our squad wasn't in the fight.

I stayed down, my gun ready, just waiting for instructions or for the enemy, whichever came first. The machine guns at the front were using a lot of bullets and within a few minutes Sargent Graham, an African American guy with shockingly blue eyes, called me forward to transport ammo to the front. I was excited and nervous all at the same time.

Foothills

Safe in the Perimeter of His Hands

Hunched over and moving forward as fast as possible I carried my M16 in my right hand and a twelve pound can of machine gun ammo in my left, having left my pack behind with the squad. I could hear bullets going over head with a tracer now and then. The Army rained four deuce mortars on the enemy, the mortars screamed loudly as they came down and exploded, making a quaking movement. There was a strange mix of fresh earth and gun powder in the air.

I looked across a small opening in the foliage and saw a creek about ten feet across and shallow. The jungle was so dense I could only see about fifteen to twenty feet in front of me. We were in a canyon with a steep hill to the front of us. Running as fast as I could I sprinted into the water and tripped on something, falling forward headfirst onto the far bank. The momentum drove my helmet into the soft soil, my head shoving into the steel pot on my head, scraping my ears and nose. After some graphic remarks, I got my head and helmet in place and turned to see what I'd tripped over.

The body of a North Vietnamese soldier had rolled face up and I was looking into his lifeless eyes. I'd seen that look in the deer I had killed in my youth. There were bullet holes all over him and blood everywhere. This was the first dead human body I'd ever seen. I must have sat there for a good thirty seconds, just staring into his vacant eyes.

"Where the hell is that can of gun ammo?" was yelled. As I moved to get up all the foliage in front of me was cut down. I could hear the bullets, see the tracers and feel the wind from the brush falling on me. Now I tried to climb inside that steel pot on my head. All that crawling the army had us do, while they fired live rounds over us, came in handy. I crawled up to the machine gun, gave them the can of ammo and crawled all the way back to my squad, going around the dead soldier, without my stomach ever leaving the ground.

There was another round of those four duce mortars going over as I checked in with the fire team leader; each squad had two fire teams. The mortars were screaming as they come down exploding the ground and sending a concussion. It was still ahead of us, probably 200-300 meters. There's a point where they either go over you or they hit you. It doesn't take long to learn the difference.

The squad leader was on the radio. Then he looked at me and said "North they need more fire power with headquarters. Get up there." We were taking casualties at the front, and they needed more men. I put my pack on and as I crawled past him, he said "wait, you have a can of ammo on your pack, we may need that". He sent up a young recruit instead.

The mortars continued straight for about five minutes before another volley of shells went over, four at a time. This volley sounded different, louder, as it came over, much closer. It hit about thirty meters in front of our squad.

The ground shook like a mini earthquake and pieces of wood, earth, and shrapnel were flying all around us. The concussion affects your ears first and then your whole body, like a wind current. It's so fast it shakes your whole body.

For a few seconds everything was quiet, no more rifle fire.

The area around us was cleared of brush and I could see up a lot farther. Then the moans and painful cries start. Men's screaming pierced the air and the desperate call for medics. There was dust everywhere and the acrid smell of explosion strong in the air.

People were stirring around, finding wounded. The dead and dying seemed everywhere. Then I saw the young man that was sent to the front in my place. He was face down with his pack still on. Someone turned him over and where his heart had been, there was a three-inch hole with lots of blood. There was blood everywhere. The shrapnel had passed through his pack, into his back and out his front. Another guy came up beside me and said, "better him than you, right?" I just nodded; not knowing what to say or how to respond.

I looked around in shock.

The smell of fresh earth, blood and human flesh hung in the air. There were pieces of bodies scattered around; men bent and bloody, limbs contorted and distorted, flesh torn and broken bones.

Twelve soldiers were dead and twenty-two wounded.

We had killed more of our own that day then of the enemy.

"Never Forget March 26th, 1968 B company 1/502 Infantry"

The daily log of the company's activities states it thus: "B Company was in the valley to the West of FSB Lyon 629223 (hill 285) in heavy contact with the enemy. An error in adjustment of the 4.2

mortar fire resulted in heavy casualties. Retired General Cushman, second battalion commander at the time, recalled this as the worst memory of his military career."

ARMSTRONG EDWIN LAWRENCE	PFC	20	26-Mar-68	B CO
BENN PHILIP CRAIG	2LT	22	26-Mar-68	B CO
DERRICO JACK EDWARD	SP4	20	26-Mar-68	B CO
GIBBLE ALVIN RALPH	PFC	20	26-Mar-68	B CO
HORTON JOHN RICHARD	PFC	21	26-Mar-68	B CO
HUBBARD GLEN DAVID	SP4	18	26-Mar-68	B CO
KREK PHILIP JAMES JR	SGT	21	26-Mar-68	B CO
KRUEGER WAYNE DALE	PFC	20	26-Mar-68	B CO
LINK ROGER MARK	PFC	21	26-Mar-68	B CO
SMITH JOE WILKINS	PFC	19	26-Mar-68	B CO
TERRY HOYLE JR	PFC	21	26-Mar-68	B CO
BARNES JOHN HOWARD	SGT	22	27-Mar-68	B CO

Chapter Three — Pure Chaos

The enemy had already moved on, thankfully, because it was pure chaos before a perimeter was set up for security. We were later told that the forward observer called in the wrong distance for the mortar drop. The forward observer has a few jobs; identifying the location of the enemy, the friendly, his own location and keeping oriented during any movement. The forward observer first determines his position and then by using distance and direction he can establish where the mortars should land.

The forward observer had brought the mortars in closer to us, instead of lowering the zone 2-5 meters he lowered it 5-0 meters, 50 meters or 150 feet. This lowered it too much, putting it directly over us and landing right on top of the headquarters group. The company commander, a captain, had an eye missing and the forward observer, a first lieutenant, was dead.

Our platoon had one squad close to the shelling and all but one man was killed or wounded. Sadly, this had happened to the survivor once before; he lived while all his buddies died around him. He was Airborne and the first squad he lost had went through jump school

25

with him. This second group were all replacements, and he was the squad leader.

After that, he would volunteer for the dangerous work without even looking back. You could tell he was really affected by the loss of out surviving all his men and he went a bit insane. He started cutting ears off the dead and collecting women's breasts to be dried and sold on the black market as tobacco pouches. He went home before I did without ever being wounded but I would be surprised if he's functioning today.

My squad leader came and asked if I had training in C-4 and detonation cord. I had, so he sent me with some others to a hilltop to start falling trees. C-4 is a plastic, putty textured explosive that burns like Sterno on steroids when lit and we used it to heat c-rations.

We wrapped the white explosive rope around the trees to blow them off their stumps. This was a terribly slow and messy process, but it gets the stumps low enough that a helicopter can hover over the brush.

It was after dark when we finally had the area cleared and start loading the wounded. It had taken so long to get them medevac'd out;

the medics had run out of morphine.

Body bags were dropped, and we began placing the deceased into them. This was a horrible job to say the least. There were body parts spread all over; arms, legs, some were so mangled we just put pieces into the bags. It was a very sobering experience. This was war, this was death.

I didn't know these guys, but they were just like me, out here to serve their country, and they lost their lives for it. It was then that I saw him.

Hank.

He was among the dead.

Hank.

The E5 I had sat next to for twenty-seven hours. We had talked and laughed together just a few days ago. I was determined at that point not to get close to anyone.

No one was guaranteed to make it out of this alive.

No one.

Hills above the rice paddies

We spent three days there cutting in a landing zone for helicopters to bring supplies. The Army also brought in people to investigate what had happened. After the panic and chaos subsided, a young man from Pittsburg in our platoon started asking 'how could this happen?' He wrote his senator, a man his family knew personally, and two weeks later he was taken out on a log bird, a resupply helicopter, and we never saw or heard from him again.

We began investigating the North Vietnamese Army's camp.

There was an ample stream with water falling over rocks, about twenty feet altogether at different spots, so the water would be cleaner for their use. The creek I had crossed during the ambush, with the dead North Vietnamese, was a small branch going into this stream. It was really a beautiful area with a four to five-foot waterfall. Everything looked lush and green, a change from the decay we had just left.

Left – This soldier came down with syphilis.
Right – This soldier lost his whole squad, twice.

The North Vietnamese had dug tunnels into the hillside for their living area and kitchen. The stove pipe was buried, running up the hill some 200 feet and then exiting in two different places. The North Vietnamese were notorious for building tunnel systems. It was their main way to store food and ammunition and to house combat and medical supplies. Tunnels could easily be 125 miles long and built to survive attacks. Sadly, most of these tunnels were made through forced labor from surrounding villages.

This particular tunnel held a printing press and lots of propaganda leaflets. We spent two days shipping out the printing press and blowing up the tunnels so they couldn't return to it.

Fire Base

The company then split into three platoons to walk out. Some of them went back to landing zone Sally. Our platoon, what was left of it after losing twelve men, some dead and others wounded, was to head to a fire base about two days walk in the Quang Dien District.

Late in the afternoon, we came to the head of a big valley. Normally in the jungle you can't see very far but, in this case, we came out on a small cliff. There was a large rock outcropping standing tall through the valley. It had a river in the center and was surrounded by steep hills. The view was breathtaking.

After all the death and destruction, we had just witnessed, it was truly beautiful.

View from Fire Base

Safe in the Perimeter of His Hands

It took a day to make our way through the valley and close to the rocks. After setting up a perimeter, the lieutenant assigned positions for the squads; he was camped at the top of the cliff overlooking the valley with two squads. My squad set up two ambush sites about 200 meters down the trail. There were two rock piles close to the trail and the squad leader assigned a fire team, five guys, to each site. The machine gun was set up to have the best line of fire at the trail.

A fire team is what it sounds like; we broke up into smaller groups to watch for the enemy. Our fire team had four members because of the casualties we had lost. Each person was to do a two-hour watch during the night, but no one was to sleep. We were on fifty percent alert which meant you could doze but you better wake up if you're needed. The way the rocks were positioned, the man on watch had to sit in a strategic place in order to best see movements.

Tom

I took my turn of guard duty in the middle of the night and was then hunkered down in my fox hole. I roused when it was just early light before dawn broke through. It was quiet, with no sounds or movements, and I looked to see who was on guard. It was our team leader, Pratt. He was sitting up with the rifle across his lap, sound asleep.

I watched for a good five minutes, moving around to look down the trail when finally, I woke him with the barrel of my M16 to the side of his head. He startled awake with a start and wanted to know what was going on. I informed him that he was sound asleep on guard duty and, although it appeared that he didn't care about making it out of this country alive, I had every intention of making it home.

By then he was wide awake and came to a stand telling me I couldn't talk to him that way. I quickly responded by reminding him that I wasn't the one found asleep while on guard duty with an M16 to the head. Everyone was awake at this point. I told Pratt if I ever caught him sleeping again on guard duty, I'd kill him myself. The training I went to said if you sleep through guard duty you can be executed.

If the enemy had walked up on us, they could have killed us all. Pratt was gone shortly after that with medical problems, and I never saw him again.

Tom and Dennis

That day our squad had to lead the platoon and I was appointed point man, the soldier who is the first point of contact and usually a few feet out in front of everyone. The point man is always on fully automatic with the guy behind him on semi-automatic, you never lost sight of the point man and if something was spotted, he would react.

The squad leader handed me a map with our position marked and asked some questions about map reading before determining that I could find the fire base. I was considered a 'fat ass leg', a term given to those who were just infantry and not truly jump school trained Airborne; I was expendable. I didn't want to take point, for obvious reasons. I thought it would be a likely way to shorten one's life span and I had no experience doing it.

I found out, however, that I was good at it. I could quickly spot the manmade things along the trail, the parts the enemy had tried to camouflage, and I was cautious about it. I had hunted a lot as a kid, and I think this really helped. I had always looked for tracks and brush being moved by the animal and found it was very similar in some respects.

The top of a bunker

The next day, late in the afternoon, we walk into the firebase. There were no roads to it, only trails. We were told we should all feel safe; the artillery on this fire base could fire in any direction for miles around any time they were needed, day or night and the entire base was surrounded by concertina wire.

Soldier on left was a replacement, soldier on right lost squad

Safe in the Perimeter of His Hands

This soldier was from the Midwest

Upon entering the firebase, we were assigned bunkers. They were just a hole in the ground with sandbags against the walls and metal plating over the top with sandbags over that. It was a twelve-by-twelve room, no furniture except a few plastic hammocks and a gas lantern. I noticed the lantern immediately; it was burning differently. I had used them before while camping and we always used white gas. I asked the guy what he was burning because it looked so strange. He said it was gasoline and it was working great.

Tom inside a bunker

Well, I had my doubts about it, because I really thought you could only use white gas in them. I continued into the bunker but chose a spot close to the door which was a distance from the lantern. There were five guys in there with one on top, hid with sandbags, pulling guard duty. We would all trade off and take turns on guard.

Inside bunker

The soldier, who was proud of his lantern, was sitting in a small plastic hammock. He was acting like he was in charge or at least in charge of the lantern. Several hours went by, some guys were sleeping, a few were talking, when suddenly, there was an explosion! I felt a huge wave of heat and saw a flash of flame before the gas impact hit me.

That damn lantern blew up!

I rolled once and then I was outside. It had taken all the hair off the right side of my head including my eyebrows, lashes and sideburns. I smelled burnt hair and felt to make sure I wasn't on fire or missing any parts.

One guy came running out on fire. I grabbed him and started beating the fire off him. Everyone else quickly pushed their way out and then the lantern guy in the hammock emerged.

The hammock had melted to him!

He continued running, arms askew and screaming, heading towards the concertina wire. I ran after and tackled him before he hit the wire and began pulling him back up the hill.

I grabbed his hand, but the skin just slid. He was burnt everywhere. His face was all black and burnt; his hair was gone, just random sprigs sticking out across his burnt scalp. He couldn't see anything and just kept screaming. I grabbed onto the front of his shirt and started hauling him back up the hill.

The medics and other soldiers had arrived at that time and with their help we got him back up to the base and the medics started working on him. He was medevac'd out shortly after that with two or three others who had been burnt badly. I'm not sure if they survived or if that guy ever regained his sight, we rarely heard anything once they left.

We were back at that fire base a few other times and I found out about satchel charges. The enemy would start mortaring the fire base, sending in about ten rounds of mortars to distract the base, while the North Vietnamese soldiers cut the wire circling the base. The enemy really relied on mortars more than we did because they were easy to carry, portable and capable of serious damage!

When the mortars stopped the North Vietnamese soldiers would then run into the base with a satchel full of grenades or other explosive devises, we called these guys 'sappers'. They would pull one of the grenade pins and then toss the satchel into the bunkers; it really was a suicide mission.

It was vital to always have a guy on guard duty. One incident we were on the fire base when the mortars started. Quickly after they stopped and the guy on duty yelled 'sapper, sapper' and we started shooting the invaders who had already cut the wire. They were inside the base and headed to complete their mission. Thankfully, we eliminated them first.

Another time we watched a chinook come in. It hooked onto a

duce and half that they used right there at the base and tried to move it. The chinook picked it up and then set it down. It did that a couple times before they unhooked it and the chinook took off. Then some soldiers pumped all the diesel out of the duce and a half. A couple hours later that chinook returned, hooked onto the truck and took off. It just needed that extra weight removed so it could haul it.

The Chinook and the duce and a half

One mission had us restocking at the firebase and then heading out. We were awaiting the log bird with our supplies when we saw it coming in from the east. We didn't hear any small arms fire, but suddenly saw the helicopter start to smoke.

They were hit!

We watched as the gunners began throwing bags out the door to lighten the load; and then we saw the rainstorm of our mail falling from the smoking log bird. The engines shut off and the chopper came into the perimeter of the fire base. As it got closer, it became apparent it was headed right toward us and I quickly took cover under a duce and a half.

The smoking chopper hit the ground hard, pushing the skids out. The rotor blade went flying and that chopper spun around, landing at an angle. I was sure that bird was going to come apart, but the crew were all safe and I was impressed with that pilot's abilities. We never did recover the mail.

Chapter Four — Supplies

Every three to five days the supplies would catch up with us and we would be issued c-rations and ammo and might be surprised with a mail pouch. More often than not, our three-day mission was extended to five and we would be short on food.

Sometimes it would be two weeks before we were issued new fatigues. The fatigues all came in one bag, it was a one-size-fits-all outfit. If you were six foot tall, they were going to be a little tight but I was 5'9" and they were a bit loose. There were ties at the waist and then the tops of your boots to keep the bugs out; no one wore underclothes or socks.

This particular time we were all sitting around, having set up a perimeter, and were repacking our bags. During these times I would help Clark, a soldier from Mississippi, write letters home since he couldn't read or write.

Some guys were napping, others eating some c-rations. One guy was listening to his radio. He would pull it out, probably once a week, and manage to pick up an American station to listen to.

The medic was packing his medical bag and for some reason

45

decided he needed to clean his pistol. Now I have to say, I had never seen him use it, so I'm not sure why he was cleaning it.

The proper way to clean a .45 pistol is to drop out the clip and then hold the pistol with your right hand, facing your left and put your hand over the top and slide it back quickly to get the shell out of the barrel.

This medic put his hand over the barrel and kept his hand on the trigger. I'm still not sure how he accomplished all that. He pulled the trigger, shooting through the palm of his hand and taking out some of the bones that work his middle finger.

He immediately started screaming.

Everyone was alert now, especially the guy with the radio. The bullet had landed between his legs, flipping the radio into the air and hitting back down hard. He came up off the ground cursing and shouting at the medic saying if his radio had been destroyed, that medic would be dead.

The medic was of course in pain and shock and had no idea what was going on. He was holding his hand, blood streaming down his arm, rocking and crying out in pain.

46

Those of us looking on thought it was sad and funny; we were in wonder that anyone could shoot themselves that way and amazed that anyone could care more for his radio than a person. But I guess looking back on it, that radio was his link to home and we all desperately wanted to make it back home alive.

Chapter Five — Village Sweeps

Villagers

We were always doing search and destroy village sweeps. It required us to search through the village for the enemy and destroy anything that the enemy could use. We would start at one end of the village with everyone in a line. The distance between each soldier would vary but you had to see each other. We would walk from one end to the other looking for Viet Cong, North Vietnamese, and weapons.

It was always good to pick up a stick and use it to tap the ground in front of you. There were spider holes everywhere; that's a hole the enemy digs to hide in during the day and then come out at night to fight and try to kill us.

Many times, a village would seem like two entirely different villages. There would be a section without grass; a well walked trail for people, water buffalo, carts and 3 wheeled motorbikes and scooters like Cushman makes. On one side of the trail would be a normal village, with houses made of bamboo and other wood or even a few concrete cinderblock homes; one or two small rooms at the most.

The other side of the trail would look unused. Sometimes it was bombed, and other times weeds and shrubs would be overgrown. But, if you looked closely, and knew what you were looking at, you could spot the signs that there were people moving out into that area. They had spider holes to hide in whenever we came looking for them and the villagers would very rarely reveal them or tell us anything.

*Someone set up this picture with the boy,
helmet, gun and cigarette. He was loving it.*

In one village I went up to a house; you didn't knock, but just pushed the door open with the gun barrel or with your left hand as you are holding the rifle close. So, I open it up and there were six or eight people sitting around a circle at a table.

I don't know any of the customs over there or anything about the religion, but it looked like a ceremony of some sort. There was a propped-up bundle on the table with a fancy looking cloth over it. I didn't know what it was, but I was ordered to search everything.

I asked if anyone spoke English. A woman said she spoke a little and I told her I needed to look at the bundle to see what it was. She said no, I couldn't, and was very adamant about that. I said again that I needed to look, and she again insisted that I couldn't. I finally got it through to her that I had to, I was required to.

I had to know what was in there.

She went over to the table, lifted off the frilly blanket and then started untying some ribbons. It looked like a giant loaf of bread at that point. She unwrapped it slowly and then I saw it.

It was a dead baby.

She started sobbing; body shaking, deep, painful cries.

I felt so ashamed and embarrassed.

I hope they understood that I was required to search every area. I told them to continue and backed out. I felt horrible about it and to this day it bothers me that I did that. I don't think they were hiding anything; I think they were just trying to honor that baby and its death.

Village women carrying supplies

Every village brought with it something new. In one village, the houses were scattered rather than in a line. There was a main trail about ten feet wide, large enough for the villagers to push a three-wheeled cart on and then trails peeled off from that. I was about three houses into the village when I met up with another soldier on the back side of one of those houses. The walls were made of bamboo and had thatch roofs. We heard a ruckus behind the house and then the wall looked like it moved. We both took a knee, our rifles ready.

Safe in the Perimeter of His Hands

The wall shook and then suddenly flattened out revealing a water buffalo looking like he was ready to kill somebody. His massive head was down, nostrils flared as he shook his head and snorted, steam rising off of him. He charged straight at us, going at least 25mph.

I stood up and emptied all nineteen rounds into him before he could clear the house debris. I glanced over and saw the other guy standing, having emptied his gun as well. I had another magazine ready to go but the animal was dead. The company ended up having to pay for it, but I was glad it was him and not me.

It was life or death in an instant with a water buffalo.

Safe in the Perimeter of His Hands

One sweep led us to a twelve-foot-high hedge row at the end of the village. The thick vegetation was intermixed with trees and bamboo making it at least twenty feet deep. To my left was a wide trail, obviously the main path used, and in front of me was an old, overgrown pathway. Our orders were to check for the enemy, and I could see that this old path hadn't been used for some time. Stepping in about a foot, I couldn't even see light through the other side. It would take hours to go through it, clearing it of any traps that might be present. I thought briefly about tossing in a grenade, but the growth was so thick I didn't bother with it and instead stepped to my left, going through on the main trail.

On the other side of the hedge was a dried rice patty where the rest of the platoon was gathering. Security perimeter was set up and most were taking the opportunity to catch a quick nap or eat a c-ration.

Following behind us was the command group including an E6, who was in his mid-twenties, and a radio telephone operator (RTO). This sergeant was always trying to point out booby traps to us and it was kind of irritating. He considered himself an expert on it although he had never actually put his hands on one. He just had this 'I know it all' attitude about the traps and it was annoying to say the least.

Everyone was sitting around, waiting for the command group to get there. Groups of guys were talking about what they'd seen in the village, some laying back on their packs resting. Others, like me, were digging into a can of c-rations. After being on high alert while going through the village, it was a nice break, if you could call it that, to be in the perimeter and 'safe' for a meal.

Suddenly a big explosion went off in the hedge row. Guys jumped up, rations went flying, and everyone rushed over. I was one of the first on scene.

It was the sergeant in the command group. He took that dense pathway that I didn't check out and clear. The explosion blew off two fingers on his right hand. He had it pressed up to his chest, screaming. Blood and chunks of flesh covered the front of his uniform.

The RTO was laying on his back, almost sitting up, with his radio on his back. There were bubbles coming out of his mouth and his eyes looked shocked. I rushed to help him, putting my hand behind his head hoping to elevate him to breath better and lift his radio off. My hand sunk into something wet and warm. I pulled it back and stared at my fingers, now covered with his brain matter and blood.

He was dead and the blast hadn't even taken off his helmet.

The grenade had to have been shoulder high because it didn't affect the RTO's radio and pack. The sergeant just walked through the line that it was tied off to and the kid was in the middle of the blast.

Emotions went through me like a roller coaster as I stood looking down at him: guilt for not checking out that part of the hedge and anger towards the sergeant for going through it. I walked over to the sergeant, now being attended by the medic. I laid into him, chewing him out for walking into that hedge when there were no signs anyone else had used that path. I told him he should have used the other one, like everyone else.

I was out of line to do that.

The man was hurt and in shock, his RTO was dead and I'm sure he felt bad about that too.

It was a bad day all the way around. There was a young man who died, and he didn't need to.

Safe in the Perimeter of His Hands

This is a community rest room with a hole in middle of the floor that has tapered concrete. A pole sites in the hole and you move it, do your business and then put it back. The bamboo pole is seen in the picture.

The enemy had defenses set all over. The most common trap was the punji pits with sticks. These pits were about two feet wide and thirty inches deep. The enemy would sharpen bamboo slits a half to three quarters of an inch wide. These extremely sharp sticks were then placed inside the pit, often tainted with feces to cause infection. They stuck up from the ground and from the sides of the pit at an angle. The idea was that a foot would drop about eighteen inches onto the sharp bamboo spikes, hitting the foot, ankle and calf. The pit would be covered with a light netting allowing sod to grow and hiding it from view.

The whole purpose was to maim the soldier, not kill him. The Viet Cong believed it was more damaging to wound a soldier, therefore effectively taking out three soldiers: the injured one and two to help him. It also set up the need for a medivac.

During one sweep in April, in the Quang Tri Province, we had two men, Ortiz, my squad leader, and Rhodes, a good friend, step into punji pits. Rhodes pit had a trip wire attached to it and before he could call out, it exploded, killing him instantly.

I helped wrap his remains in his poncho for the medivac.

Any death is hard, but Rhodes was close to everyone in the squad. He had enlisted and joined the Airborne. He would often tell us about his dad and the department store he owned in Portland, Oregon.

Safe in the Perimeter of His Hands

Ortiz

Ortiz didn't have any other lines attached to his pit and we were able to get him out of it. The sticks went into his foot and ankle, and he was painfully lifted away from the pit and medevac'd to the rear for medical treatment. He was back a few weeks later having recovered from it.

The combat boots we were issued were made for the rugged environment and provided some ankle stability and lots of traction. They were suited for the jungle and its wet terrain; in the way they were made. The boot was made of canvas from the ankle up and helped to prevent jungle rot. There were one-way drains on the side in the arch area to allow water to flow out and the boot to dry.

The army discovered a flaw in the make of these, however, in the fact that they provided absolutely no protection from the punji pits and the sharp sticks would go through the sides and soles like a knife through hot butter.

The design was improved, and a steel plate was added into the bottom of the boot.

Tom in a village

During one sweep three of us and a medic came to an enemy spider hole that had a lid on it. We shoved the lid off and yelled "từ chối" which is "give up" in Vietnamese. No one responded or came out, so we opted to toss a grenade in.

Our medic asked if he could toss the grenade, and not seeing a reason why he couldn't we agreed. We instructed him on how to cook it first: pop the pin and then say one, two and throw on three; you have three to four seconds before it blows. Well, the medic popped it, yelled "fire in the hole", threw it into the hole and we all watched as it immediately came back out of the hole.

The three of us instantly hit the ground flat with our heads the farthest from the grenade. The medic, on the other hand, got down on hands and knees with his butt towards the hole. The grenade blew and all that shrapnel peppered the medic's butt cheek; he looked like hamburger. He was flat on the ground then, moaning in pain.

We were still in danger. One soldier crawled over to help the medic and, ironically, started calling out for a medic while the other guy and I crawled back to the hole. I immediately fired a magazine of bullets into the hole while the other guy cooked a grenade and threw it in.

The medic was medevac'd out after that, but the mission wasn't over. We called for a tunnel rat; that's a guy who crawls into the hole, after making sure there aren't any booby traps around the entrance and hauls out all the bodies and whatever else he finds in there. This particular soldier was a small American and he was good at his job. He took a .45 pistol and a flashlight with him, crawled into the hole that was no wider than his shoulders, and began pulling bodies out. There were usually one or two women in each spider hole as well as the North Vietnamese.

The spider holes were a whole network of tunnels and holes. Imagine an ant farm if you will, all their tunnels dug into the dirt and going various ways. This was the same concept except they could have multiple entrances, a kitchen, vent holes, ammunition dump, a food and first aid area and so on.

Clearing the tunnels took time and patience. I respected the tunnel rat a lot. There's no way I would want to crawl down in there. When they started looking for one, it was always the smallest guy they could find, I would will myself taller. That was the last job I wanted!

Safe in the Perimeter of His Hands

Buddha Temple

There was one soldier, a big husky Samoan whom we all called Pineapple; he was a really neat guy. He was one of the original Airborne, but he didn't treat those of us who were replacements any different. He was easy going and friendly to everyone and everyone liked him.

We were going through a village on a sweep, and he was two guys over from me. One minute we were walking along and the next minute he was blown up. He walked into a booby trap tied to a grenade and it blew off both of his legs and a hand.

He didn't scream or cry out but seemed in control. I'm not sure if that was because of the shock but, for what he lacked in panic, the medic made up for.

The medic was new and extremely nervous about all the blood and loss of parts. Pineapple just reached over and put his hand on the medic, telling him to settle down, reassuring the medic he could do it; he'd been trained for this.

That was quite a sight; a man bleeding from both leg stumps and his severed arm, reaching out and comforting another.

It's a picture that has always stayed with me.

The medic gave Pineapple morphine and put a tourniquet on both legs and his arms to stop the bleeding. He was medevac'd out shortly after that and we heard later he survived two days before dying at the rear.

He only had two months left of his tour.

The boy on the right studies at the Buddha Temple

One soldier in my unit was a full blooded Native American. He was in his mid-twenties and although he had joined the army, he wasn't Airborne. He loved being called Chief. During one village sweep we were walking along when Chief tripped a wire. He actually saw it as he pushed against it and yelled out 'trip wire'. I was there first and followed the line, finding where it was tied off to a grenade pin. I secured it and he was able to get out of the danger and we destroyed the trap without any mishap.

Had he gone any further he would have pulled the pin and set it off. It could have killed him. After that, he was always my buddy.

Chief

We took over part of a village during one mission. We swept through the village and then asked one of the villagers if we could set up camp on his front lawn. We were there two or three days and swept the village numerous times.

I remember the family being extremely nice. Three generations lived there, the grandparents, whom I asked permission from, their son and his wife and their grandson and granddaughter

The family made me a tray of food, which I ate. I experienced dysentery for years after that meal but I remember thinking how little they had and yet they prepared that for me. It was really touching.

I felt bad for the villagers; they wanted our help, needed our help, but they were there in the war, living with it daily, having it knock on their door and destroy their lives.

The tray of food the family made me

The Grandfather whom I asked permission from.

This is the grandmother; the table in front of her is actually the bed, unmade.

Second and third generation. The guy on the left is a professor at the University of Hue, he's about 40.

The villagers house

This is the front area we camped at. The guy in the middle is from Guam; one time he climbed up a palm tree, after several guys had tried and failed. He took a machete with him and just scaled up the tree like it was nothing. He then proceeded to cut down several coconuts for us.

Tom

Front – Nakquin, left – Bob Sweeney, Center – Tom, Right – Clark

Chapter Six — Lighter Side

About midday we came upon a small pond that had a creek running into it on one side and out of it on the other. It a beautiful little area and we set up a perimeter to take a break.

There was an older man in a small boat out in the middle fishing. We sat around eating our lunch and watched him for the longest time, not catching anything.

Finally, I had our interpreter call out to him, saying that I would help. I popped the pin on a grenade, cooked it a second, and tossed it into the water. The concussion sent the fish, at least twenty, to the surface and the man was instantly happy, yelling out his thanks and began scooping them up.

I got in trouble from my sergeant for that stunt because I didn't yell out 'fire in the hole' but the man's family ate well that night.

Safe in the Perimeter of His Hands

The man and his boat

We rarely got to take in the beauty of the land as we were either in a fire fight, on patrol, or on duty, always alert and on guard for our lives. I do remember one time coming around a bend in the trail and seeing a small deer ahead grazing.

It didn't look like any of the deer back home. It was tiny in stature, beautiful and peaceful, something so very foreign in this war-torn land. It was a good reminder that this land was beautiful and not everything was out to kill us.

The Army tried a new form of c-rations one time. They were

made in Albany, Oregon and were a dry pack of food. Unlike the c-rations, that were all in cans, these lightweight packs were supposed to be easier to carry, lighter. You just had to heat water and rehydrate the food.

When they pulled them out, I grabbed a chili con carne and went about heating my water over some C-4. The pouch was about 3 inches squared. There was a cardboard bottom with a plastic bag attached, with the food. You could open it up, sit it on the cardboard bottom, and just pour the water in.

It looked like a dry soup mix while I poured the water in. The directions said it only had to sit a few minutes and then I would have chili. I waited and stirred. Stirred and waited. The water eventually got cold and yet nothing ever softened. The 'beans' were still little hard pebbles. I honestly don't think even a jack hammer could have softened the mess.

I discarded that and opened a can of c-rations instead.

When we were done with our c-rations, the ends were cut off the cans and they were then flattened and just discarded; it's odd to think of how many cans were probably left across Vietnam. If we had left them as a can, it would have been a ready-made bomb – just put it over a grenade and add a string.

One mission required us to be flown via helicopters to our new location. We began taking on fire and the pilot said he would hoover above an open hill as we jumped out. I looked out at the steep hill as guys started jumping, I barely had time to register the vertical grade when I jumped and landed facing downhill.

I just started running.

It was that or roll, and I knew I didn't want to do that with a hundred-pound pack on my back. It wasn't long before I realized I would be on top of the enemy if I didn't stop and would have to crawl back up the hill.

I quickly put on the breaks and fell down. The fire fight ended soon after that and we continued our mission.

It's funny to think back on, I could have ended up running right through them at the speed I was going.

Another time we had to jumped out of the helicopter and landed in elephant grass. The helicopter was hovering about five feet above the top of the grass; we didn't realize it was about ten feet deep.

Once we jumped, we just kept falling. The temperature, after dropping down in with our packs on, increased at least twenty degrees.

Elephant grass is very hard to walk through and could easily hide a unit for an ambush. It almost made you feel claustrophobic with its closeness, as if you were suffocating. It's extremely high and dense, like a clump of bamboo with sharp edges. We were all cut to shreds by the time we walked out of it.

Looking out of the helicopter, Sergeant Graham

It was extremely hot out one day as we were coming out of the jungle and into an area with a stream. It was wide and at least chest deep; as the guys in front of me crossed they would come out of it and then throw up, each one. I wadded in and felt the extreme cold against my very heated body and my stomach immediately started cramping. I felt sick in an instant and sure enough I trudged through the water and emptied the contents of my stomach on the other side, along with all the other guys.

One morning we found ourselves in the deep jungle and it was fairly easy walking. I was on point and had my machete in the left hand with the M16 laying on my ammo pouch which was attached to my belt; that was the usual way to carry a rifle. I was cutting a pathway through the undergrown because you never took an established path; it was guaranteed to be booby trapped.

As I cut through some vines, I saw a spider web in front of me, spanning the six-foot width of the pathway I was making. A spider was sitting in the middle of the web; it was so big my hand couldn't even cover it.

It was huge!

I moved to the left and the spider seemed to turn and follow me. I eased to the right and again he followed.

I instantly flashed back to training in Tiger Land and seeing a tarantula in the pine needles. It had jumped ten feet sideways!

I had no idea what this spider was capable of doing and I just froze, staring into all its eyes.

The guy behind me called up saying, 'The Lieutenant wants to know what the holdup is.' I responded with 'there's a big spider across the trail'. I just stood there, looking at it, when the message came back up the line 'well knock the damn thing out of the way and let's get going'. Keeping a healthy distance, I hacked a trail about ten feet long around the spider and continued in my original direction.

When we made our destination, I sought out the guys who were at the back of the line and asked them if they'd seen that spider. They all had very colorful remarks about its size and assured me that no one had moved it; it looked at each person as they walked by.

I really liked this but couldn't figure out how to ship it home.

The season was either wet or dry, but it was always hot and humid. One minute it would be pouring down rain and soaking us and then twenty minutes later it would stop, and we would dry out. The Army decided to issue us rain gear, it was thick rubber and really uncomfortable. If you were wet when you put it on you never did dry out.

I didn't have my gear for long before I realized it was just a waste of time and space in my pack. The next village we hit I traded it for Pepsi on the black market.

One night, during that constant wet season, four of us were pulling guard duty. We were across a rice patty, facing a village. It was pouring down rain, not really cold but because we were out in it so much, we were chilled.

The four of us were huddled together with a poncho pulled over the top, trying to stay halfway dry as we took turns pulling guard duty. In the middle of the night I hear, "you SOB, I'd kill you for that normally, but it's warm."

One guy, rolling over during the night, had to pee and not seeing what he was doing, had urinated on the other guy's leg. It shows the kind of situation we were in where warm pee on your leg felt good.

Tom in rain gear

That next morning, as the light was breaking across the rice patty, we watched a whole line of villagers walk out on the dike, pull down their pants, butts toward us, and proceed to do their morning constitutional. They finished and stood, pulling up their pants without wiping anything. We all kind of looked at each other and I figured a little pee seemed small after that.

We were single file, walking on a small pathway with a bluff to one side and rocks on the other. It was definitely some rough jungle terrain. I was somewhere in the middle of the line when a guy, about five ahead of me, suddenly did a header off the bluff; he went head over feet about a hundred feet down. Keep in mind we are all wearing our packs; I think he just got off balance and over he went.

Regardless of how it happened, we had to go down and get him. Removing our packs, we set up security and several guys scrambled over the edge to reach him. He was screaming out in pain and every time we touched him, he screamed louder. We figured he must have broken his back and sent a couple guys ahead to look for a landing zone.

As we worked on tying two ponchos together and moving him onto it, our search party radioed back that the landing zone was about a quarter mile away. We picked him up carefully and started forward, I remember carrying him with my right hand on his leg.

It was a slow process. Every time we took a step he would cry out and moan.

It took us two hours to get him to the landing zone and loaded onto the medivac. We thought for sure we would never see him again. Then, about ten days later, a log bird came in with supplies and off steps that soldier.

You should have seen the shock on everyone's face! Turns out he threw a disc and after seeing a chiropractor, he was just fine and sent back to the front.

Guy on the left was the one who fell off the trail.

This guy was always smoking pot and some of us joked that he didn't even know he was in a war.

We found a cache of weapons inside this house. Tom is on far right.

Safe in the Perimeter of His Hands

Bob Sweeney was one of those guys you just really wished wasn't in the Army. I'm honestly not sure how he even made it through training before being sent to Vietnam. This guy would constantly get heat exhaustion.

We would be walking along when he would start to stumble on the path and veer off to the left or right. You could instantly tell that his whole demeanor had changed, and he just wasn't in control of his faculties. Everyone learned to recognize the signs, and someone would call out, 'Sweeney's hot again'. At which time we would look for water, set up a perimeter and then two guys would take him into the water, dunk him down, walk him, dunk him down again; it was a cycle. We were there for at least an hour, dunking him in the water and then after he was cool, checking the three guys for leeches.

On the off chance there wasn't water close by, we would dump canteens over his head and find some shade. The medics said there wasn't anything they could do, either for him or for getting him out. It was usually ninety degrees or hotter, so dipping Sweeney was an everyday occurrence. We all looked forward to the monsoon rains, just to give us a break. It would rain for twenty to thirty minutes and then quit, then start up again about three hours later. It was just enough to keep him cooled off.

Thinking back, it was a wonder we weren't ambushed one of those times, just trying to keep Sweeney alive. It was a bit of a lighter side, all of us pulling together, spotting his exhaustion and dealing with it.

We were given iodine tablets to put into water.

The formula of water to iodine was such: running water was 1 tablet, brown water was 2-3 tablets and thick and lumpy water was 3+. I shudder now to think of the water quality we consumed but we didn't have a choice. It was fill up when you found water, not search for the clearest and cleanest supply.

Chapter Seven — Permanent Ambush Sites

November 1968, Tom at An Lo

Every three to four months we would end up back at the permanent ambush sites set up along the paved, two-lane Highway One and stay for a week or better. There were three bunkers, each large enough for a squad to fit in, just north of the An Lo bridge; they were working on the bridge the whole time I was there. The highway

ran north to south, and the river ran east to west.

I can remember being there several times and a few interesting

things happened while we were there.

Village women walking along Highway One.
These women, who were very small of stature and didn't weight much,
could balance these sticks and packs and make it look easy. The GI's
wanted to try it one day, and a guy fell over.

Safe in the Perimeter of His Hands

We were given one hot meal a day and if we weren't pulling guard duty, we could walk along Highway One, through a village, and get it. I was stationed at the bunker the farthest north and we had to walk a click (kilometer) or click and half to get there.

We were told we could carry our weapons and ammo, but the guns were not to be loaded. Well, I was in a war zone, and I chose not to follow that command.

One day a few of us were walking down to eat. Command dictated that we do the buddy system but there was a guy, about fifty yards ahead of us, from another bunker, who was walking alone.

Each side of the road had rice paddies spread out and villagers were working, as it was the wet season. To the right was a kid sitting on top of his water buffalo. Sometimes the buffalos would eat the grass that grew on top of the dikes.

Suddenly that buffalo stuck his head up, started sniffing and curled his nose. Then he looked at that lone GI and started shaking his head. The buffalo took off up the bank, about ten feet, toward the highway. The boy fell off as the animal charged up the bank.

The GI looked over to his right and started to pick up his rifle, which he realized wasn't loaded, and then jumped to his left into the wet rice paddies and tried to outrun the buffalo.

The buffalo at this point had raced up the incline, crossed the road and was starting down the other side, right behind the GI. I quickly ran to the side of the road raising my gun, along with the other guys, and we emptied our weapon into the enraged animal, dropping it before it could get the soldier.

The GI had fallen face first into the rice paddy and the dead water buffalo slid down the hill next to him. We helped pull the guy out and he went back to the bunkers to get cleaned up. It was kind of funny but could have meant death for that soldier.

The company required we report what had happened. No one was reprimanded but the Army sent a representative out to talk with the villagers, who were very upset about the death of their animal and reimbursed them for it. The Army had told us, at some point, that we were not to shoot at the water buffalos unless absolutely necessary. I was personally involved in the shooting of two of these animals and both times were life and death incidences.

Safe in the Perimeter of His Hands

Kids watching over their water buffalo

One soldier, Ferguson, was messing around with a M72 Law, it's a long fiberglass tube that has an eye site. You put it on your shoulder, site it and then shoot. The rocket goes out the front with a blast of exhaust out the back.

Ferguson was standing in the large doorway of the bunker with his shirt unbuttoned and his helmet off; remember the bunker is made out of sandbags. He was really kicked back, and I think a little bored, so he decided to shoot the M72 across the rice paddies.

I was about fifty yards away with another group of guys. We

were sitting around talking and watching him with the Law when one guy says, "He's not really going to shoot that from the doorway, is he?" About then he shot it.

We didn't even look at where it landed, we were too stunned that he had shot it from the bunker doorway. That back blast had swirled around inside the bunker, ripping apart the sandbags and sending all the sand toward the door, where Ferguson was standing.

That sand blasted the shirt right off him and removed part of the hair from his head. It truly was a sand blast all over the back side of him. He was raw and red from his scalp to his butt. There were lots of jokes going around about him after that. Guys would say things like "we have to shoot this law over here Ferguson, would you like to stand in front of that brick wall for us". We were there for a week, and he kept getting salve from the medics to put on his back and head. He never lived that one down.

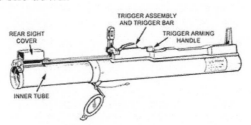

Drawing of an M72 Law

The An Lo bridge in construction behind me.

Another time, while at the bunkers, we were given Pepsi.
Everyone had two or three six-packs per person as it came in on a big
pallet. It was about 90 degrees out and so was the temperature of the
Pepsi.

Someone said that there were ice trucks, DeSoto trucks, going
up and down Highway One so we decided to stop one and get some

ice. We flagged down a 20-foot truck with a covered box on the back, all shut up. We waved it over and opened the back to reveal the ice.

The excitement was palpable as we saw all those cold bricks, just the thought of that cold Pepsi was paradise. Then we heard the voice of a woman who spoke better English than most of us. She said something like "By what authority do you men stop us?"

We looked at her in shock before someone finally said "Well we don't have any authority to stop you, Ma'am, but we have some hot Pepsi and would like some ice. We can buy it from you".

The businesswoman in her kicked in and she said, "If you're willing to buy it then you are willing to trade some Pepsi for it, right?" We all agreed. At the end we had a block of ice and she had Pepsi for the black market.

Left to Right – Clark, Charley, Graham (behind), Ortiz (front)

Tom and Dennis Rose.
Dennis lived on a houseboat in Florida with his dad.

Safe in the Perimeter of His Hands

The latrine was a little bit out from the bunkers. It had sandbags built up with boards, basically a sandbag for each cheek, and was at sitting level. The cat hole was sixteen inches wide and about two feet deep. It went on for ten to fifteen feet; we just kept moving it as it filled up.

I went out one morning, after we had recently moved it, and was sitting down doing my business when suddenly, the boards broke. I was thankful the hole wasn't full as I slipped down into it. My back was against one bank with my shoulders wedged in and the backs of my thighs against the other bank, my butt was down in the hole with my knees against my forehead.

I was stuck!

I started yelling for someone to come help me. Several guys came at a run, spurred on by the urgency in my voice. Then when they saw me, pants around my ankles, butt in the cat hole, they started laughing. A few turned back to get cameras shouting to not move till they got back. I thought to myself, if I could move, I wouldn't have hollered for help. But remained there till everyone had their picture and they hauled me out. I'm probably in someone's photo album somewhere.

Kids were always begging for food

I was in line one day for the hot meal when a helicopter flew
over, bars out on either side, spraying something. I'm not sure what it
was, a bug repellent or agent orange, but you could see it coming
down, like sheets, and settle over the top of us. It felt sticky as it
landed upon my bare arms.

I made it through the food line, which was outside and
exposed, and dumped my tray at the end. I was in it enough; I didn't

need to ingest it too. I walked back to the bunkers and opened some c-rations.

Agent Orange is an herbicide/chemical combination that was used as part of a chemical warfare program, Operation Ranch Hand. It was widely used for the ten-year span of 1961 to 1971, during the war. Apart from damaging the environment it was later found to cause major health problems. Research shows that the South Vietnam President, Ngo Dinh Diem is actually the one who first requested the United States to spray herbicide on his country. President Kennedy authorized it in November of 1961.

During that ten year span the US sprayed nearly twenty million gallons of chemicals. The goal was to knock down all the foliage and eliminate any area the enemy could hide, making it easier for the US military to attack. It would also wipe out any food source that the enemy had. What they didn't consider was how it would affect the villagers. It was sprayed on them too; the innocent people we were there to help and protect.

By 1970 over eighty five percent of the crop lands in the Quang Ngai province were destroyed, contributing to extensive famine; leaving villagers malnourished and starving. That year also led to some medical research being done. It was discovered that South Vietnamese women had high doses of dioxin in their breast milk and that US military from Vietnam had it in their blood. This led to birth defects in offspring both among the Vietnamese and American children. While I was in Vietnam, they told us the Agent Orange was harmless and we shouldn't worry about it.

I have four children and they all suffer somewhat from it, whether it be displaced hips at birth or stomach issues as they grow. I believe it is all related to Agent Orange, but the US government doesn't recognize it as a reimbursable issue. Sadly, the decision to spray mass quantities of chemicals in 1961 is still affecting people in 2022.

Swimming at An Lo

An Lo Bridge

We were paid with military payment currency or MPC. It looked like Monopoly money. Every few months the army would change it out, so if you were using green, now you might have purple. If you didn't exchange it to the new color, then you couldn't use it.

I was walking through the village, on my way to the exchange, when a villager stopped me and asked if I could exchange their money as well. They had $50 of the current color. I assured them I would and headed to do just that.

Afterword, I waited in the village but didn't find them. I tried again the next day, but again didn't see them. I ended up with an extra $50 that month.

At An Lo the trucks drove across the river until the bridge was completed. The stakes marked the 'road'. The water was waist deep.

Chapter Eight — My Twenty-First Birthday

May 22, 1968

Morning broke through the trees on May 22, 1968. The day was warm but not overly hot and the platoon was up at daybreak to take in all the trip flares and claymores. The Lieutenant wanted the 1st squad to make a two-kilometer recon, two clicks, up a dried creek bottom.

The squad of ten men divided into two fire teams, a rifle team and a machine gun team, and started out about an hour after daybreak. The squad leader told me to take point. Now normally I wouldn't have thought twice about walking point but today was my twenty first birthday and I thought it would be a terrible day to die.

We started walking up a creek that ranged from fifty feet across to 125 feet. It was a beautiful area, with big full trees covering the entire width of the creek. Now the creek was basically dry other than a few spots of water two to ten feet across.

It was different than any creek I had seen. There weren't any rocks on the bottom, and it didn't have high banks. It was like the

104

water could follow the lay of the land. There were no farms or villages in this area, it was just a big valley in the jungle with vast open spaces.

We continued walking up the creek. The beauty of the tree covered area with the sun rising over head, penetrating the leaf cover, gave it an unreal feeling. It was hard to believe we were in a war zone.

I began to feel ill at ease, like something wasn't right. I moved over to a big tree and stopped to look. The squad was spread out behind me and stopped to wait; you could always see movement the best by not moving. I had seen birds in the trees earlier but now there weren't any. Nothing was moving anywhere.

Then suddenly from the left, I saw a bird fly out as if it had been disturbed. About two hundred feet ahead crossing the creek left to right were six North Vietnamese.

They hadn't seen us yet.

I dropped onto my stomach and when I was sure the last man had entered the clearing of the creek bed, I opened fire.

The rest of the squad started firing and immediately the North Vietnamese returned fire. It was all over in a matter of seconds.

We had got the jump on them.

A search of the bodies showed one officer and five enlisted men. They had AK47's, ammo and a supply of food. We took it all with us, including their belt buckles, and left the bodies. I kept two of the belt buckles as a souvenir, which I have to this day.

Later, after completing the 2 click recon, we rejoined the platoon. That night we set up a new ambush site with the trip flairs and clay mores. I felt a sigh of relief that I had made it through the day.

I've definitely had better birthdays but that one will forever stay with me.

Chapter Nine — A Lunch of Mortars

Like the last mission, we were split into two fire teams, one with a machine gun and the other a grenade launcher, and we were leading the platoon; I was with the machine gun team. We formed two lines about twenty feet apart and each man was about ten feet from the guy in front of him. We were walking through a dry rice paddy and to our left, down an incline, was a grouping of foliage so thick we couldn't see into it.

Suddenly there was a lot of machine gun fire and we quickly got down. We couldn't see it hitting anywhere. Then I heard a weird sound to my left and looked over; the soldier was just standing there in shock. His jaw was hanging off and part of his tongue was missing. Guys rushed to help him as the medic was called over.

The sergeant of the platoon said "North, you and Blaisdale go over and start toward that forest line. Looks like that's where it came from". Chuck Blaisdale was new to the company, having just been transferred in and we had become friends. He was from Portland, Oregon.

We stood up and started walking toward the trees, holding the

M60. Chuck said "Is this how the company works? You attack with an M60?"

I said "It's a new one on me. I've never done it. But if there's even a hint of fire towards us, get down! I'm not running towards it!" He said he wasn't either.

Then we heard a mortar sound and stopped. It hit off to the side. The Lieutenant said to stay where we were; they would send in a squad to recon and take out the mortar position.

We just sat down and, figuring it was going to be a bit, took out a can of c-rations. We were talking and eating and could hear those mortars going off. Pretty soon one hit behind us about 100 feet. Then a minute later it landed less than a hundred feet in front of us. We look at each other and I said, "You know what just happened?" and he said "Ya, we were just bracketed."

Quickly, we got up, lunch forgotten, and ran diagonally 100 or 150 feet back from the forest and toward our left. We heard the mortar launch as we were sitting down and turned to see it hit exactly where we had been sitting.

At the time Chuck and I laughed at it. But if we hadn't moved,

I wouldn't be telling this story today.

Tom in the jungle

Chapter Ten — A Shau Valley

The A Shau Valley is west of Hue along the border of Laos. The valley runs north to south and is about twenty-five miles long and about a mile wide with tall elephant grass throughout. It is flanked by two mountains covered in dense foliage and is part of the Ho Chi Minh Highway that the enemy used to move materials and men from North to South. It was a well-used and effective means of transport for the enemy.

While on recon in the valley, one day, we had the platoon, over thirty guys, walking in a sump area with a hill to one side of us.

The Lieutenant got a call over the radio telling us to evacuate the area; there was a big group of North Vietnamese just over the hill headed straight for us. Command said they had two helicopters available to move us but only one could land at a time.

We set up a perimeter for safety and listened to the radio, waiting for a rescue. Everyone was on full alert, and you could cut the tension with a knife.

The first bird landed but they could only carry three guys at a time. The gunner said it had to do with the heat or the air inversion.

110

Whatever the reason, they were only transporting three guys at a time. And so, we waited. The first load left and then five minutes later the second bird landed, and three more solders boarded.

I know I wasn't in the first load. I'm not sure how we picked who loaded first but I remember standing there, scanning the area, waiting for the enemy to pop out. Every time the helicopter left, they would go out of sight and then eight to ten minutes later the other one would return. It was one of the longest, most terrifying waits of my life.

It took over ten trips to get everyone, but they got us out and moved to safety. We never did see the enemy that day and I was grateful.

While walking point, I came to an open spot that was about two hundred feet across. I immediately stopped and took a knee.

Something was wrong.

The leaves, across the clearing, were turned wrong; the underside was up.

Everything looked boxy, built; it was an ambush site.

I called Lieutenant Cody up and explained what I was seeing but he couldn't see what was wrong. I explained that it wasn't natural, and it had to be an ambush site.

Cody finally complied and sent a fire team to investigate. A short while later they radioed back that it was indeed an ambush site all set up. They destroyed whatever was there before coming back and we continued on. No enemies were sighted, but we destroyed their hovel.

While on recon in the triple canopy, we needed to communicate our location to a helicopter. There was so much foliage, it felt like we were in a hole, sunk in under the thick triple canopy. The dense thickets of bamboo made every step a chore, chopping our way through.

The pilot had to know where we were in order to drop something to us. I honestly can't remember what it was that he was dropping, but to find us, we had to pop smoke. That's a canister you hold and once the top is popped, a colored smoke comes out.

For identification purposes, we would pop the smoke and then the pilot would radio what he saw. So, we popped orange and he radioed purple. We told him negative and popped green. He then identified orange.

We were immediately told to pull out and that mission was aborted. I'm not sure what was going on, but we began the trek out of there without completing the mission.

Viet Cong prisoners of war

Sitting in a fox hole, 100% alert, the air was filled with tension. It had been a tense day, we lost a few guys, and I was feeling my mortality as I sat there, gripping my weapon. I suddenly looked up at the night sky and said to myself, "I don't know if you are really up there God, but I'm going to talk to you. I won't promise to follow you, but I will look at your book and give it a fair chance when I get home. I could really use your help now to survive and get home safely."

I'm here to tell you God is real, and He alone is the reason I'm able to write this today. He knew me before I knew Him, and He loved me. He wrapped His arms around me and brought me home. All the glory and honor are His.

Chapter Eleven — Hue

We were rotated to Hue, the imperial capital city of Vietnam, to do some security at the harbor. Hue is located along the Perfume River and is about five miles inland from the South China Sea. Geographically it is basically in the middle of Vietnam with the river cutting the city into north and south and was about 60 miles south of the DMZ, the demilitarized zone.

Hue University

Safe in the Perimeter of His Hands

In January of 1968, during the Tet Offensive, Hue was captured and held by the North Vietnamese Army for almost a month. It was recaptured by ARVN and the US in the bloody Battle of Hue where the North Vietnamese lost about 5,000, the ARVN lost around 2,500 and the US lost 1,800 soldiers. Approximately eighty percent of Hue was destroyed during the battle and thousands of civilians were killed in the crossfire or from the North Vietnamese Army.

It was an easy job doing security and honestly a nice break from the jungle and the enemy. We were there for a few days and were able to restock and rest up a bit.

Hue Harbor; we were there to guard for a few days.

Hue Harbor

Chapter Twelve — Lieutenants

I had three lieutenants while I was in country: Reeder, Hayes and Cody.

I remember one mission with Lieutenant Reeder, we were in the underbrush, which would be comparable to the vine maple and rhododendrons that are in Oregon. Walking through it required a lot of machete work. As we were coming up out of the underbrush the radio telephone operator received a call asking where they were. Reeder's response was 'We just come out of Marlboro Country'. His response wasn't well received on the other end, but we all had a chuckle.

It was under Reeder's command when we captured one of the enemies and held him as a prisoner of war (POW). The prisoner was naked with his elbows tied together behind him. I remember opening some c-rations and sharing with him.

It was radioed in that we had a POW and the captain on the other end replied, very point blank that no, we didn't take any POW's today. Reeder then told the interpreter to take care of it. The interpreter is the one who did it because then we, the US military, wouldn't be held accountable for the prisoner's death; it came at someone else's

119

hand, no matter who commanded it.

The interpreter walked over to the man and told him, in Vietnamese, that he was going to kill him. He then proceeded to shoot him three times in the genitals, probably hitting his spine. It made me sick witnessing this murder because that's what it was. This man had surrendered, he was in our care and because someone in the rear didn't want to deal with it, he was murdered inhumanely.

Lieutenant Hayes was around for about two months He had been an E6 and went to officer school. He called us Hayes Hogs and his wife actually made us black scarves to wear (you can see it around our necks in most of the pictures). He was a gutsy guy and I liked him a lot.

On one mission we had been hit hard and had four or five guys wounded. Naquin was one of them. He was injured really bad, with a hole in the left part of his chest. We were taking turns on perimeter and watching the injured guys. One soldier and I sat next to Naquin, talking to him and trying to keep him calm.

The other guy asked if he wanted a cigarette and he said, 'I can't smoke, I've got a hole in my chest' to which the guy responded, 'well, then you don't have to worry about exhaling.'

Naquin

The attack had happened close to sundown, and it was after dark when we were able to establish a perimeter and call in the medivacs. We were in the dry rice paddies, but it was too dark for them to see where to land so Hayes walked out in the middle of the landing, with a flashing strobe on his helmet, to direct the helicopter in; I was on perimeter duty.

That took balls!

It was scary to say the least since we weren't sure if the enemy was still waiting there for us or if they had moved on.

That helicopter came into land and its tail section hit on the dike. The tail went straight up in the air with the nose down and I thought for sure we were all goners, that it was going to take us all out. But that pilot was good! He just spun it around and sat it down, aided by Hayes light. We quickly loaded the wounded and got them out of there.

Tom

Safe in the Perimeter of His Hands

The final lieutenant was William Cody, he had reddish hair. His dad had a military career and Cody was an Airborne Ranger. It was with him that we had a rifle inspection. We were back at landing zone Sally, our headquarters, and he told everyone to clean their weapon for inspection.

Now the correct way to clean an M16 is by first disassembling it and then cleaning away any carbon buildup and, per the instructions, lubricating it before reassembling it and presenting it for inspection; you had to recite your weapons serial number.

I never put oil on my guy because it would cause it to jam and misfire. Instead, I had a shaving brush I carried with me and that's how I would clean it. Well, Cody wanted it bright and shiny. He told me I didn't pass the inspection and said, 'North you're the best guy I got in the field but you ain't not worth a damn back here."

I was told to do it again, disassemble, clean and reassemble for inspection. I went to the armory and talked with the guy who was in charge of it, he had previously been in my squad. I told him I needed a new gun and after he issued me one, I memorized the serial number and then went back for my inspection and got a 'good job, North'.

He liked having me walk point, but a squad leader couldn't walk point; he made me a team leader instead to get around that.

Chuck Blazdale told me that sometime after I went home Lieutenant Cody had stood up in a fire fight and 'John Wayned it', meaning he shot from his hip, and was killed. He always loved being called Wild Bill.

Chapter Thirteen — Things Are Not as They Appear

It was the dry season and extremely hot. The morning light was trying to overcome the darkness of night as our platoon walked through a large endless field with trees on both sides. Each step kicked up more dust. We were hugging one side, along the trees, and I was walking point.

As we rounded an outcropping of trees, I saw a Vietnamese farmer. He had on white shorts and shirt, like most farmers wore, and was digging. I stopped to watch him. It looked suspicious because there were no plants around and he was digging his hole in a shaded spot.

The man was intent on his work and didn't see or hear us. I walked a course that put the farmer about fifty meters to our right. When I was about 100 meters from him, I saw that he was covering up a hole.

The farmer looked up with surprise and fear at me. He dropped the hoe, turned and started to run, he had about ten feet to the tree line. I started shooting and so did the guy behind me. The 'farmer' dropped to the ground dead.

The lieutenant, who was several guys behind me, came to the front and started chewing me out for shooting an innocent farmer. I looked the lieutenant in the eye and told him, 'Let's talk after we dig up what he planted'. With that the lieutenant told the soldiers to set up security while five of us walked over to the hole.

One guy picked up the hoe and began to dig. About two feet down he hit something and reached down to pull it out. It was an AK47. There was also a canvas backpack with a pair of boots, the black uniform of the Viet Cong, two hand grenades and two 15-round clips. The man had been a farmer by day but an enemy by night.

The lieutenant looked me straight in the eye and said, 'Good work North, now let's get on with the mission.'

Village in rice paddy area

About two weeks later we were ordered to do a line sweep of a village that was abandoned in the foothills. We went into an area that had recently been bombed. There was a lot of destruction; mounds of earth and deep craters, uprooted and broken trees.

Just outside the village was a spring fed pool. We walked around some debris and there, standing in the pool, were at least 100 flamingos. The sergeant commented that they would look good stuffed. I was just amazed that in this war, in all this destruction, these

127

beautiful birds existed.

We continued into the village, each man about twenty feet from the next guy online; we were spread out walking side by side. We were walking along, tapping the ground looking for spider holes or booby traps. Within the first 200 meters, two soldiers were killed from booby traps. The lieutenant had us pull back and set up a perimeter around much of the village. He then called in a medivac for the dead soldiers and called an air strike on the village.

Two jet fighters from the navy carriers in the Gulf of Tonkin flew over. Each jet made three runs dropping two bombs each pass. It was late in the afternoon at this point and the lieutenant said he didn't want us in there after dark, so we kept our positions around the village all night on 100% alert.

Day light came with no movement or sign of life from the village. The lieutenant ordered another air strike, so I took the opportunity to have some breakfast and cracked open a c-ration. About mid-morning the lieutenant said we were entering the village but instead of sweeping we were doing it defensive position. This meant I was point man going in first with two guys behind me.

Safe in the Perimeter of His Hands

Very slow and careful we started into the village, my rifle on fully automatic. This time everything looked different with the broken houses and rubble everywhere. Based on the debris you could determine there had been a variety of houses: bamboo and wood products and then cement and cinder blocks.

There were bomb craters all over. They weren't as deep as the ones created from the B52 bombs. These bombs had come straight down and blew a large hole. There was a rise in the road, it went up fifteen to twenty feet. As I got to the top, I saw movement to the right and quickly went down on one knee with my finger on the trigger. Through a pile of wood debris, I saw the movement again, it was a woman, a mother, poorly dressed in tattered clothing, with a little girl about four or five who was barely covered and shaking from fright, cold and hunger. The little girl was holding as tightly as she could to her mother.

I called them over, not knowing if it was a trap, and they quickly and eagerly came to us. We called the medic up and interpreter. He asked them about the village, if the enemy was hiding anywhere. She said it was just the two of them, and it was. We gave them food and a poncho to wrap in and kept them with us for the day. That evening they went out on a helicopter to the hospital.

They were the last ones in the village and appeared to be shell shocked. It was sad to see how the villagers were affected by this war. These two had taken a beating and survived.

After we found them, we continued walking over the rubble and avoided any trails in case the booby traps had survived the bombing. I would take a few steps and then stop to look. It was almost impossible to walk the rubble and look around. Therefore, the process went on for hours. Once we started in, we had to complete the walk through the village as there was no safe place to stop. Tension would begin to build among the troops, and everyone was ready and often expecting the worse.

As we continued walking around an enormous bomb crater, it must have been twenty to thirty feet across and at least twelve feet deep, I heard the whoosh of two mortars being launched. I immediately jumped into the crater, thinking I would be less of a target, and stayed face down waiting for them to land.

I heard the 'whump' sound of them landing in the distance and rolled over to look around. I was startled to see twenty other guys and the Lieutenant in there with me!

I chuckle about it now, thinking back, but if a mortar round had exploded in the middle of us, I'm not sure how many medivacs it would have taken to extract the carnage.

Tom has frag grenades hanging off his belt and a bandoleer (magazine full of ammo)

Chapter Fourteen — Combat Infantry Badge

The platoon was out on a mission, it was in the evening, and we had a secure perimeter set up with a big circle of fox holes. A log bird came in with supplies and dropped off an E7. For reference's sake, we will call him Walker. He had been in the army for ten to fifteen years and was in his early thirty's. They said he was there to get his combat infantry badge (CIB).

We were all slightly confused by this announcement. The CIB was something you earned by being in combat, not something you went out to the field to get. The best description I have found is in "The Psychological Effects of the Vietnam War" by Josh Hochgesang, Tracye Lawyer and Toby Stevenson. They said it this way, "It is a small, simple blue badge worn by the members of a very exclusive fraternity. This fraternity isn't academic or athletic or dedicated to making money. Yet, the admission standard was very strict. Not all the members of this fraternity wanted to join, but every single member paid the same dues. The cost of membership was easy to understand. To belong, you had to be willing to kill other human beings and the only way out of this club was to die or go insane. The school was the

University of South Vietnam and graduation was a bitch.

The United States Army awards the Combat Infantryman's Badge to infantry soldiers who served in a combat unit, line crew, fire team or in some other combat compacity during a time of war. Maybe it isn't the most famous medal or award, but it is the most honored. Only the Medal of Honor is worn above this beautiful, hard symbol."

So, with confusion, we accepted Walker into our midst. We unloaded the supplies and realized he didn't even have the proper gear to be out there. He had web gear and a little pack. He was all decked out and looked like a new recruit; I think there were even creases in his fatigues.

He stated that he wants to get in a fox hole and "get on with it". We put up firing sticks to mark the firing zone, it could be a ninety-degree shooting window depending on where the other fox holes are. The sticks allow you to recognize the enemy from the friendly. There were two to three guys per hole, and I was in the fox hole to the left of Walker.

During the night we all took turns on duty from our fox holes. It was Walker's turn to pull duty when suddenly there was a grenade explosion in the fox hole directly to his right. There was an immediately sound of pain and men crying out. Unsure of what was going on we crawled over to that hole to help. One man was gut shot and he bled to death right there, his hand grasping his mid-section, blood and internals covering the front of him.

The other two were bleeding too but still alive. We lifted the wounded men out among their cries of pain and the medic went to work trying to stop the bleeding and save their lives.

The first fifteen minutes after the grenade went off were chaos as we tried to find out what had happened. Walker kept saying 'I thought I saw something'. He never came out and said it, but we knew he had tossed a grenade over and close to that fox hole. There hadn't been any trip fires, nothing to warrant a grenade toss without warning. He just threw it over there.

It could just have easily been thrown into my fox hole.

The explosion killed one soldier and seriously wounded two others. The medivac was called in, but it didn't arrive until morning. The medics worked on keeping the men alive and as pain free as possible till the evacuation.

Several members of the platoon banned together and started talking, stating that Walker had murdered that soldier, which he did. Everyone was upset and things were being said like 'first chance I get, he'll be in my sights'.

He left on that medivac. He claimed he was defending us, but he knew his way around the Army. Whether it was ignorance or on purpose to claim his CIB, he killed a man and possibly the other two, who didn't have to die.

On Patrol in the foothills. We don't have our ruck sacks on.

Crossing a foot bridge. Clark is at the end.

Chapter Fifteen — Body Count

The platoon was tasked to search a village along the An Lo River. Immediately upon entering we started taking on rifle fire. We were ordered to pull back a reasonable distance and our position was radioed in with an airstrike request.

It didn't take long before we saw the aircraft fly over and release two napalm bombs. One hit its mark but the other one hits the ground and bounced. It went up in the air, flipping end over end and headed straight toward us. Someone yelled 'Get down' and it flew over our heads, dropping to the ground, but not going off. We all sighed a sigh of relief when it didn't explode.

The jet then made another pass and again released two bombs. The same thing happened!

One exploded with rolling black smoke, fire and then white smoke and the other flipped end over end to land behind us, not blowing up but just sitting there.

When we saw the second coming at us you could see guys whispering prayers and doing the sign of the cross. We had been witnesses to the devastation napalm did to a body, I can't even imagine what would have happened if those had gone off.

Of course, we couldn't just leave them there, we had the task of blowing them up! After attaching C-4 and a blasting cap to them we retreated to a safe distance and set them off. We could still feel the heat from the explosion! I was later told that they didn't blow upon landing because the bombs weren't activated when they were attached to the aircraft.

There were a variety of smokes over there, the frail grey smoke was burned rice fields. Brilliant white smoke meant phosphorus and the deep black smoke was napalm; it would suck the air right out of your lungs.

Safe in the Perimeter of His Hands

It took a few days and several fire fights to clear the village and then we had to search through it. It was a miserable job to say the least. Part of the village was destroyed from the bombing; houses were mangled along with bodies.

We were into the dry season but found a stash of weapons the enemy had buried while it was wet. One soldier found an AK47 with dried mud on it. He knocked the dirt off and pulled it back to cock it saying, 'look, this thing still works' and then pulled the trigger.

It was a stupid move to make.

It shot over the top of another guy's head, who had his helmet off, and was facing the guy who fired it. The dirt from the barrel hit him in the forehead. It didn't break the skin, but it caused his forehead to get red.

The guy started shouting 'you shot me' and cussing at the guy who was still holding the AK47. Everyone else started laughing because no one was hurt.

The searching continued throughout the next two days. There was a graveyard and we had to dig up any fresh-looking graves to determine a body count. The company was running a contest to see who had the largest body count, the winning platoon would get a 'kick back' and go to the beach.

I dug up two graves and they were civilians, not soldiers. We ended up finding several civilians who had died and been buried recently. We reburied any we found.

The village, as I said, was next to the river. One guy saw something in the river and after looking closely we could see that eight to ten feet out were bodies. The heads were visible just under the water's surface. The enemy were trying to conceal their dead so we wouldn't know how many of them we had killed but as the body's filled with gases they floated to the top.

The army called in the Navy divers, and they cut the bodies loose. The bodies, at least a dozen North Vietnamese soldiers, were weighed down with ropes and rocks. The Navy divers' drug them to the bank where we hauled them onto the shore. They were discolored, swollen and decaying. It was disgusting, there's no other way to explain it, dragging them out of the water. We just left them there on the bank to rot after we counted them.

The contest ended and our platoon won the highest body count and received a three-day kick back to Coco Beach. It had permanent barracks right along the beach. There were surf boards available, and I tried my skills at surfing. The waves were small, and I could lay on my belly, paddling out into the ocean pretty far before getting up on my knees and rowing around for a bit. When a little wave came by, I would turn the board and jump to my feet, usually falling over sideways.

The board wasn't attached to my ankle, and I would have to find it after going under. I tried about six times before deciding surfing wasn't my forte. I couldn't even stand up for ten seconds.

It was a nice break from being at the front and we were all enjoying it. That evening we went to some entertainment, there was a band from Australia. I remember them singing the song 'Wild Thing' but they would change the lyrics to fit the GI's. The next day we were back trying to surf and just relaxing on the beach.

Safe in the Perimeter of His Hands

Evening entertainment

Halfway through the second day we got notice to suit up; beach time was over. We were going in where another platoon, one from our company, had run into a real problem taking on fire. The platoon, located in some white sand dunes near the coast, was tripping so many mines, the medivacs were having trouble keeping up.

We were told that the current platoon couldn't walk out because of all the booby traps. The Army took a chinook and landed it where it was sandy but not really in the sand dunes and extracted that platoon with their wounded.

Then they dropped us off via Huey's!

I'm still not sure what the logic was behind this maneuver, none of us understood it. If it was that bad for them then why were we going in?

It was midafternoon when we were dropped at the new location. It got dark around 6pm year-around. We were told to continue the mission and the Lieutenant, William Cody, told me to take point. That was the slowest walking point I had ever done, painstakingly slow. It's one thing to walk point and quite another to walk knowing there could be land mines all over.

I had a stick and poked around in front and to the sides of me before taking a step. Everyone, all thirty, stepped in the same steps. Some guys were in panic mode, and you could hear other guys talking them down, telling them to keep walking. It was after dark when we finally made it out and could claim we were safe from land mines. We were never fired on and didn't hit any booby traps. It was just a mission of stress, endurance and team bonding.

That was the end to our contest winning kick back. We never did get to finish our time at Coco Beach.

White sand dunes with fresh water. Chuck

Chapter Sixteen — 100% for the Night

One mission involved the whole company, about a hundred of us. We walked to an area and the company was dug in in a circle. Four squads were sent out and mine was directed to go out 1,000 meters and set up an ambush; these four squads would be the first line of defense.

After finding high ground we set up and called in our marking rounds. It was about eleven at night when the guy on guard duty, Dennis Rose, who was using the night vision scope, the starlight scope, said he could see the enemy moving around down below us.

We could see where the company was dug in, someone would light a cigarette every once in a while, and you could hear them coughing. We, on the other hand, were quiet and had no lights.

The enemy was visible between us and the company although they were closer to us. We called in our positive sit rep (the situation report was called in hourly and a report of negative was given, or we would state the problem for a positive situation) and got permission to fire. We would be firing toward the company, so they were told to get down. We started firing in a rotation, about fifty rounds per minute.

148

We were awake all night, 100% alert. Throughout the night the company would send up flares so we could see better.

At daybreak we ceased fire and the company sent out a squad looking for the enemy. They didn't find any, the enemy must have crawled out during the night, but we had done our part.

Tom with the starlight scope

Incidentally we were told that the starlight scope was brand-new technology and to be careful with it. It was considered state of the art technology then and weighed about 6 pounds. We were told that under different circumstances, we would have had to have a high security clearance just to handle it.

I was carrying the scope one day as we were crossing a little bridge; it had thin poles on the sides to hold onto. The scope was in a green case that was supposed to be waterproof. Well, I fell in and the Lieutenant said, 'hand me the scope'. I was still in the water, mind you, up to my chin. I put up my hand and told him to help me up first, so they did. Once out of the murky depths we opened the case to discover it wasn't waterproof and dumped the contents before we continued on.

The scope was really a delicate thing in the way we had to handle it. It came with a lens cover that had to be used at all times because light would scar the lens. If a flair was sent up to see the enemy, or a plane went over to take a night vision picture, there by lighting up the whole area, the scope had to be quickly covered.

Despite that, we did use that scope a lot, until we lost it.

Still not sure what happened.

Chapter Seventeen — Torture

During one mission we were planning on going into a village at daybreak. That evening the interpreters, squad leaders, point men and team leaders met with the lieutenant to discuss information from headquarters. I was a team leader at the time and remember looking around and seeing a lot of extra interpreters. Its normal for each platoon to have three or four, but there were at least ten and most of them I had never seen before.

The village was laid out in such a way that the sun would be coming up at our backs. We were to use two squads, twenty guys, and the interpreters. When the order was given, we marched out and approached the village at daybreak. I had my team on the right side, with a fire team entering on the left; the fire team didn't end up seeing any action.

There were rice paddies with dikes to the right of us and as soon as we came in, two North Vietnamese were spotted running along the dike. We quickly laid down a line of fire, dropping them both. We continued walking in and saw one North Vietnamese running out of the village about the time he shot at us. One soldier said, 'he's mine' and shot off three shells, one after another, from a grenade launcher.

The first fell short and the second hit the North Vietnamese on the shoulder, flipping him into a handstand. We could see his feet straight up in the air.

The shell had blown his head and shoulders off.

After doing a sweep of the village, we didn't come up with any North Vietnamese. We began pulling all the villagers from their houses and putting them in a central area. There were probably thirty to forty people. One woman in particular stood out. She was wearing makeup, in her early twenties and had nice straight teeth. Most villagers had black teeth or teeth that were heavily stained from chewing the betel nut, a fruit of the areca palm.

This woman was holding an infant of just a few months. The interpreters brought her over to us and started asking where her husband was. Our intel told us he was a unit commander for the North Vietnamese Army, and he brought her along to the villages where he would hide out. She refused to talk to us, just standing there, staring at us.

One of the interpreters wrangled the infant from her arms, thrust it into my hand and told me and another guy to follow him into one of the houses. You could hear her screaming at us to bring back her baby.

The interpreter told us to keep the baby crying and then he exited the building. It wasn't hard to keep it crying, it wouldn't stop. Two soldiers, more comfortable with a rifle then a baby, awkwardly held the small screaming bundle while the others made the woman talk. With each new squeal of her baby, her firm resolve to stay loyal to her husband weakened and finally she pointed out a man in the village who was in communication with the commander; he would run back and forth to give the commander information. The man was trying to blend into the background but didn't run when the soldiers advanced toward him. We gave the hysteric woman back her baby and focused our attention on the man.

The man wasn't talking, and the interpreters immediately started the torture techniques. They ordered the village women and soldiers to cut up chili peppers (these grew plentiful in gardens) and put them into jugs of water. The interpreters put the man on a board, put cheese cloth over his face and held him down while slowly pouring the chili water over his face.

I was told it gives the sensation of choking to death. They would pour some and then demand answers. When the man refused to speak, they would continue the torture. It was extremely hot out and chili water only added to that. By the third gallon and the second hour, his face was puffed up and his eyes were swollen shut. I was holding onto the guy, one hand on his shoulder and the other on the cheese cloth. The guy was stripped to the waist and his chest looked bright red. My hands were red and sore from where the water sloshed onto them.

The interpreter told the man this was how it was going to be for the rest of the day, then they would stop to make more chili water and begin again. He continued saying that this was how his life was going to be until he told us where his commander was hiding.

The man held out for six hours.

He kept the secret for six hours, endured the torture for six hours before he told us he would us show where the commander was hiding.

After that the interpreter stopped pouring the water and we let the man rest for an hour, allowing him to recuperate some. He was given food and clean water and supplies to wash his face. After the hour he was able to see out of his eyes better.

The interpreter had told me that the old way of torture was to cut off a finger or something, but that made people think they were going to die anyway, and they didn't need to give up the information. This way, with the constant chili water over them, they had to suffer, and it worked.

Graves

We had radio telephone operators in contact with the rear and radioed that we were going to a big graveyard. It was off in the distance, but we could see it from the village. Two helicopters landed near us and a colonel stepped out of one with his camera man. Two guys with backpack flame throwers jumped out of the other helicopter.

Our prisoner pointed out the opening of a tunnel in the graveyard. After it was opened someone shouted down the command "từ chối" or give up. We could hear them talking down there but no one came out or gave up. The command was given again, with no response, and then the order was given to use the flame thrower; this was the first and only time I ever saw a flame thrower used. Those two guys stood about ten feet from the hole and shot the flame right into it for a full minute. There was no sound after that.

I was grateful, once again, to be too big to be the tunnel rat. The smell of burnt flesh was already coming up from the hole. We had to send for someone to come in for that job. They ended up pulling out 8 North Vietnamese from the hole. Some weren't burnt that bad, but they had died from lack of oxygen.

The colonel received a silver star for that mission.

Graves

Chapter Eighteen — Insects, Rodents and other Catastrophes

There were dangers everywhere! Between the enemy and the landscape, you had to be on guard constantly. One such danger was the two step Charlie. It was a small bamboo pit viper snake with hemotoxic venom that would cause necrosis and death. It was said if you got bit you would only take two steps before dropping dead.

One afternoon we had set up a perimeter and were kicking back and relaxing. I was reclining on my ruck sack talking to a guy and munching on some food. There was another soldier asleep just a few feet from us.

As we were talking, we watched a green snake crawling above us. It wasn't over a foot long. Suddenly it dropped between us and the guy sleeping! "Snake" we screamed. That GI was up and running before we made it to our feet.

There were pests everywhere, sleeping, eating, walking. You were always being bit by something. One morning I went out to take down a trip wire. There had been a typhoon and the waters were about waist deep. I had to wade in and felt something crawling up the left side of my rib cage. I instantly felt a sharp stinging and lifted my shirt to find a very large centipede. It hurt for days and I had to put ointment on it from the medic.

This is the type of centipede that bit me

Rats were always in the bunkers; they would get into the walls. It wasn't unheard of for someone to get bit and then they had to have rabies shots, a series of thirteen, one a day, to the belly. I was never bit but I saw guys who were.

Flies. I don't think I ever saw a bee but there were lots of flies. You could always tell when a new guy came in, he would open up two, three, even four cans of food at a time, setting them around him within easy reach for a four-course meal. It didn't take long to draw the flies and soon those cans were covered with flies, and they were eating the food faster than him.

An experiences guy would warm his rations, one can at a time, with C4 and then gulp it down. When we had pound cake and peaches, I would break it up into the peaches, soaking up the juice and down it; that was actually my favorite.

Mosquitos were everywhere; morning, afternoon, evening. It didn't matter. They came in swarms big enough to pack you away. Several soldiers came down with malaria and had to be sent to the rear for hospitalization. They Army issued us insect repellent by the gallons, and we would carry it in small white bottles. Some said that the North Vietnamese could smell it, but honestly it was wear it or get eaten alive. I think we all bathed in it. Interestingly enough, the mosquitos don't really bother me that much anymore.

There were two kinds of leeches, as if one wasn't enough. There was the land leech and then the water leech. The land leech was everywhere, moist jungle, lowlands, and the higher mountains. When the leech bites it injects an anticoagulant into the victim's skin to prevent the blood from clotting, allowing a continuous flow of blood for it to suck on. The wound could continue bleeding for a few hours after the leech was removed.

Most days, regardless of if you walked through water at the beginning of the day, we wouldn't take time to leech check each other till later in the day. When we did take time, everyone would strip down, check each other over and help remove them. It wasn't uncommon to have four to six of them across your back and chest. Both kinds would back out of the skin once they were sprayed with insect repellent.

Later in the day we would check each other for leeches.

During one ambush we had set up the clay moors and trip flares and we were divided into four groups of four. Each group was twenty to a hundred feet away depending on the lay of the land.

It was dark out; everyone was settled in and some starting to doze off if they weren't on guard duty. Suddenly we heard some rustling noise and murmuring; then a soldier jumped up and started stripping, increasing the urgency in his tone and began slapping at his arms and legs.

We quickly found out it was red ants; he had laid down on the edge of an ant hill. I ended up with two or three bites while I was trying to get them off of him. We got him on his knees, quickly stripped him out of his clothes and got all the ants off of him. When we returned to the platoon, we got salve from the medic for the bites. They were vicious little things.

But the bugs weren't the only things you had to watch out for. Some of the guys like to indulge in the local communities and frequent the prostitutes, which there were plenty of. One guy in our squad came down with syphilis. He told me that the Army was sending him to the Philippians and he would stay there till he was cured; they weren't letting him go home infected.

Chapter Nineteen — The Death of a Friend

Ray Kriskovich

Tom and Ray

Saturday, August 10th, 1968, started out as any other day.

We were still in Thua Thien, South Vietnam. Our mission of the day was to travel to a small bombed out village that bordered a dried-up rice paddy and clear it for spider holes.

164

Safe in the Perimeter of His Hands

We arrived there at approximately one in the afternoon and swept it, finding very few spider holes. The Lieutenant had us continue on up the trail several clicks and then we doubled back to the destroyed village at about 5pm. He wanted us to dig in and set up a perimeter.

I remember thinking that we were there too early; especially since we had already been to that location today, and I voiced that to Lieutenant Cody.

He waved off my concerns and we continued to set up a perimeter with fox holes. I was digging a foxhole with my friend Ray Kriskovich, a guy from Canyonville, Oregon. I remember when he had joined our company, he had only been there about a month, and we had instantly clicked. He had walked in and said, "Anyone here from Oregon" and from that day on, we were friends.

We paused in our set up and tossed my camera to another soldier, Ray's machine gun assistant, and he took some pictures of us. The wall in the background, of the picture below, was my foxhole. Each guy was twenty or so feet from the next. Bob Sweenie was to the left of that wall.

Tom and Ray

By seven, everyone had settled in and several were relaxing. I was sitting next to the wall, my gun leaning against me, and a freshly made cup of hot coco in my hand when I heard a noise and saw a flash.

I thought to myself, 'that looks like an RPG', about the time it hit. The concussion and heat knocked me down on my gun, the hot coco went flying, and I popped up firing.

I heard Ray below me firing the machine gun.

I could see his tracers in the dark night.

So could the enemy.

Another RPG was immediately fired and landed directly on Rays position, effectively halting his machine gun fire. I couldn't hear anything from over there, we were all still firing into the night until the lieutenant called a cease fire. The medics were ordered to help the wounded, but everyone was to remain 100% alert.

Sweenie started moaning from his position behind me and called out for a medic; his shoulder had gotten torn up from the blast and was in a lot of pain.

Then I heard Ray's assistant cry out for a medic.

Ray was dead.

The RPG had hit directly on his position. The assistant was severely wounded but alive.

That morning the medivacs came, there were eleven wounded and one dead. Sweenie was taken and we didn't see him again; I hope he made it home after that. Ray's assistant went on the chopper too and of course Ray.

I helped put Ray in his poncho liner that early morning.

It was one of the hardest things I've ever had to do.

It was a heartbreaking day.

Any loss is hard; you fight among these men and no matter how hard you try not to get attached; you do. We were brothers in arms, fighting side by side, seeing the destruction, the loss, the horrors together.

It's hard to describe the loss you feel when only an hour before we had been laughing, talking, and digging alongside each other and then morning comes and I'm wrapping him in a poncho liner.

Greif is so different on the battlefield.

I don't think I ever really mourned him at that time, that came later. It came when I retold all these stories, that anguish, sorrow, loss.

It just takes longer in the war zone, but that heartache comes out.

My friend Raymond Kriskovich, I miss you!

Kriskovich is in the poncho lining on the left.

Chapter Twenty — Blown off a Tank

Later in August we were back at An Lo Bridge. We were charged with guarding four D7 cats, nicknamed Roman Plows. They had big scaffire blades on them; it was a straight blade with teeth that stuck down below the blade two feet or better. Their purpose was primarily to destroy villages so the enemy couldn't dig back in.

Safe in the Perimeter of His Hands

Six tanks would form a perimeter around the cats and then the infantry would walk as an outside perimeter to the tanks. We usually walked for a couple hours and then set a perimeter while the cat's worked. We would watch for enemies, although we never saw any, and generally it was an easy day. We did this for about five days.

On that fifth day we stayed out later and the tank commander in charge decided he wanted to get back to base faster, so he told the infantry to get on the tanks. Each tank could hold a fire team. We all found our seats on the turrets, that's the top box part of the tank that pivots. I was on the right side of the turret.

It happened to be the dry season, so as we went across the rice paddies. We would go up over the dike and then back into the paddy, up and over, back down. It didn't take but a few minutes for me and my fellow infantry to realize the commander had us going back the same way we had traveled that morning.

I remember looking at the other guys and one commented that we were going the same way. It was a rule of the infantry, and

172

honestly a rule I still follow today: whatever trail you take there, you find another one out. You don't want to return on the same route because the enemy might have set up booby traps after you walked through.

No sooner had we realized what the tank commander was doing when two explosives went off almost simultaneously. One under the track and the other under the left side. The blast, 2-105 rounds, threw everyone off. I ended up fifty feet from the tank. Everyone was briefly knocked unconscious, and it turned out I was hurt the least. I had shrapnel sticking out of my leg from the knees down.

Tom facing the camera

The other tanks had stopped at this point and people were coming to help. I was dragged over to one of the dikes, my pant legs were rolled up and a bandage wrapped around my legs and a gun was thrust at me. I was told to hold guard until the medivacs arrived. That's when I noticed I had blood running out of both ears and dripping off my chin. Someone was trying to talk to me, and I couldn't hear him, everything was muffled and ringing, all at the same time.

Tom, propped up to guard

At some point a guy shouted and said "North, I think I found your camera" and he took this picture of me. When the medivac arrived, I was put by the door gunner because the medivac was so full of stretcher cases. I remember being really cold as we went higher up and then I knew I was going to be sick and threw up right in front of me. The door gunner didn't appreciate that at all.

When we arrived at the MASH unit I was put into an air-conditioned tent and was immediately freezing. I had become so climatized to the constant heat and humidity that I was shaking from the cold. I'm not sure if I was in shock or if it was just the cold, but in my mind, I wasn't doing good.

Hospital

It wasn't long before the medics starting walking through the units asking for volunteers to move out of the air conditioning; they had casualties coming in who needed it. My hand quickly shot up and I was moved. Shortly after that they gave me a local anesthetic in my legs and cut the shrapnel from my right shin. It stayed sore for twenty some odd years, I could hardly touch it.

They wrapped my leg but left the wound open and I was sent to a hospital by the beach. After the first day they removed the gauze wrapping and stitched it up. It was really hard to walk because the skin was pulled so tight, but it did get easier.

Movie theater at the beach

One of the soldiers I met in the hospital.
He had the plane pictured below. We hung out quite a bit
while I was at the hospital.

Several days later I had to remove the stitches. I remember

walking down a hallway and finding scissors in a disinfectant jar. I cut and pulled out each stitch. I was at the hospital, and therefore the beach, for two weeks before I received orders to go back to my unit.

I enjoyed walking in the sand on the beach, a beautiful white sand. It helped heal the jungle rot that had been plaquing me most of my time in Vietnam. We didn't wear socks and the constant wet to dry to wet that our feet endured resulted in open sores and blisters. Mine didn't have open sores but the heat and exfoliation of the sand really helped clear them up.

When my orders came through, I had to hitch hike to get back to my unit. I went down south to Bien Hoa. Once there I passed a captain who was driving a colonel in a jeep. The captain slammed on his breaks and said 'you didn't salute' to which I responded that I was sorry, I didn't think about saluting, and then I proceeded to salute them.

Tom

Safe in the Perimeter of His Hands

The captain immediately started chewing me out, stating they were officers and deserved the respect of a salute. The colonel, however, asked me what I was doing and when I responded that I was 101st Airborne traveling to join up with my company after being injured, the colonel said 'you boys have been through a lot. You don't salute in the field, do you?' and when I said no sir, he responded with 'that's good, that's what we want. You go on, you're doing a good job'.

Safe in the Perimeter of His Hands

I caught an airplane that was going back to landing zone Sally, a transport plane. They hauled jeeps and trucks. It was a four-prop engine with two engines on each wing. We were told to hang on "we've never landed on this field, and it might be a little bumpy".

About that time there was screeching of concertina wire against metal. We were bouncing around back there like ping pong balls. When they let the back down, I couldn't get out of there fast enough, I was in infantry and not use to such exciting rides.

I looked around. The plane had gone all the way through landing zone Sally and ended up at the very end of the airstrip with the nose buried in the concertina wire.

I had been put on light duty by the medic and had to pull KP duty. One day of that was all it took before I told the sergeant that I felt good enough to go back out. He gave me a waver and told me to catch the next log bird and go rejoin my squad.

I was back in the field.

Tom at LZ Sally

Chapter Twenty-One — Sergeant Testing

Chuck and Tom

Sometime around September 1968, Chuck and I were told to report to LZ Sally for our E5 exams. We had to wait for a supply chopper to land and then catch a ride to the landing zone.

LZ Sally with Chuck

I really should have been squad leader before this time, but I was good at walking point and my commanders had wanted me to stay as point man. An E5, noncommissioned officer, typically isn't point man. I did still walk point though. I felt better relying on me, rather than someone else, to stay alive.

Safe in the Perimeter of His Hands

Chuck

Tom

Safe in the Perimeter of His Hands

Chuck and I both had to take written tests and do an inspection on a soldier with his rifle. The mock inspection revealed candy wrappers in the guy's ammo pouch. Different 'traps' were set up that we had to find in order to pass the inspection part of the test. We both passed and became sergeants.

We were given bunks to sleep in and hot food that we didn't have to heat over C4. It really was the Ritz in a war zone besides the mortar and rocketing that frequently occurred. I felt safer in the field than at the LZ.

This is outside the front gate of LZ Sally.
The Army paid local village women to fill sandbags, it was cheaper than having soldiers do it.

At some time, I was also interviewed to be a LRRP, long range reconnaissance patrol, but I turned it down. I thought that would be too dangerous and I wasn't going to volunteer to die. One guy I was interviewed with was excited to take the position and he was killed a few weeks later.

The LRRP was an elite team usually comprised of five to seven men who would go deep into the jungle to observe the enemy activities without initiation contact. They would then report back their finding.

Chapter Twenty-Two — Time for Some Rest & Relaxation

I received a notice that I was eligible and actually overdue to take R&R; you had to complete thirty days in country to be eligible. It was Christmas Eve, 1968. I could have stayed around to see Bob Hope or go to Hong Kong. I chose Hong Kong just to get out of the country.

I hitchhiked on a helicopter from LZ Sally to Da Nang and then waited to board a plane down to Bien Hoa Air Base. Bob Hope was playing at Da Nang and I could hear the music and cheering from the show. I didn't want to leave the airport in case I missed my flight and ended up waited most of the night for the prop plane to take me to Bien Hoa.

AIRLINE PASSENGER TICKET, BAGGAGE CHECK

AND

MAC BOARDING PASS

MISSION NUMBER	BOARDING TIME DATE	BOARDING NUMBER	ORIGIN/DESTINATION VIA	BAGGAGE PIECES POUNDS
F2B4	TIME	67	HOA XUU	No.
	DAY MO YEAR			Lb.

The Following Constitutes A Statement By the Carrier Which Is Hereby Delivered To the Passenger At the Carrier's Request

CONDITIONS OF CARRIAGE AND ADVICE TO INTERNATIONAL PASSENGER ON LIMITATION OF LIABILITY

Passengers on a journey involving an ultimate destination or a stop in a country other than the country of origin are advised that the provisions of a treaty known as the Warsaw Convention may be applicable to the entire journey, including any portion entirely within the country of origin or destination, that in most cases limits the liability of the carrier for death or personal injury and in respect of loss of or damage to baggage. For such passengers the convention and special contracts of carriage embodied in applicable tariffs provide that the limit of liability for each passenger for death, wounding, or other bodily injury shall be the sum of U.S. $75,000 inclusive of legal fees and costs, except that, in case of a claim brought in a state where provision is made for separate award of legal fees and costs, the limit shall be the sum of U.S. $58,000 exclusive of legal fees and costs. The carrier shall not, with respect to any claim arising out of the death, wounding, or other bodily injury of a passenger, avail itself of any defense under Article 20(1) of said Convention as amended by the Hague Protocol signed September 28, 1955. The names of carriers parties to such special contracts are available at all ticket offices of such carriers and may be examined on request. Additional protection can usually be obtained by purchasing insurance from a private company. Such insurance is not affected by any limitation of the carrier's liability under the Warsaw Convention or such special contracts of carriage. For further information please consult your airline or insurance company representative.

The airport for Hong Kong was on the peninsula, we flew over the city and dopped onto the airstrip. It was the weirdest landing I had ever experienced. Several years later I watched a TV show that said Hong Kong airport was one of the most dangerous and challenging airstrips, unbeknownst to me.

When I landed in Hong Kong, I was strip searched.

That was a unique experience!

They were looking for drugs and everyone on the plane was searched.

I had reservations at the Presidents Hotel, located on Nathan

Road, the main access. It was a popular spot for the military to be. It was lined with restaurants and shops and had a constant stream of people, day and night. I remember having a hard time sleeping because of all the city noise; it was always active. I also found it interesting that there were no stop lights anywhere.

We were given some R&R tips before we left country including establishments that were out of bounds.

OUT OF BOUNDS ESTABLISHMENTS

1. ALL TATTOO PARLORS
2. ALL BROTHELS
3. CHAMPAGNE BALLROOM
4. {ALL GUEST HOUSES IN
   {CHUNGKING MANSION
5. CHINA ART EMBROIDERY CO.
6. *Le Lucky Bar*
7. *The International Tailor*
8. *King Tailor*
9. *[illegible] Custom Tailor*
   [illegible] Tailor

I looked at the booklet on the flight and found it very informative. "So here you are in Hong Kong, one of the world's greatest vacation spots with 5 days to spend. Be sure to spend them wisely and well by taking time out to do some sightseeing and to take advantage of Hong Kong's shopping facilities (with suitable precautions against being gypped). Over 4 million people are jam-packed here making it the world's most densely populated area. Minority groups of Americans, British, Portuguese and Indians lend the city a truly cosmopolitan atmosphere."

It also had some humous areas, "If you find yourself in a car with a WHITE license plate, get out. They are illegal and you are not covered by insurance."

"Money does not grow on trees so be careful with yours."

"Night life and then some!! A lot of hotels have their own night clubs and all of them have fine restaurants. There are specialty restaurants all over the Colony with very reasonable prices for what they offer. Remember, we said night clubs and not "girlie bars.""

"Only carry enough money around with you to take care of that day's needs. The rest of it you can safely leave in the Hotel lock boxes which are provided for your protection. Beware of pick-pockets and those lovely hostesses who make a handsome living separating you from your cash."

Safe in the Perimeter of His Hands

I had my parents wire me money since my Army salary, $90 a month, was given in Army payment currency. It looked a lot like monopoly money; I had actually borrowed money from Clark before I left Vietnam.

I'm not sure if I ever paid him back.

I had to go to the Western Union to pick up the money from my parents, which was located across the bay in Kowloon. I took the Star Ferry to Kowloon and then got in a taxi and asked the driver to take me to the Western Union.

The driver drove for at least ten minutes before stopping. I stepped out and looked up at the Western Union sign. I turned around and, across a large parking lot, was the ferry I had just gotten off of.

Boy did that driver see me coming!

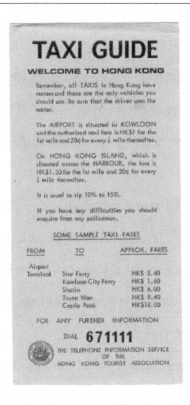

Back at my hotel, I was taken to an 'escort service' and assigned a girl. It would probably be considered a tour guide in today's times, but we called them escorts. There was a line of girls, all Asian, and I just picked a pretty one. They were all in short skirts and looked 'American' in dress.

That first night we ate in the dining room in the President Hotel, it was a large area with go-go dancers and a band.

Safe in the Perimeter of His Hands

The next day she took me to a movie theater close by and we watched *Bullet*, staring Steve McQueen. The theater was massive with balconies and alcoves. It reminded me of the theaters I would see in older movies. When we entered my escort chose our seats off a diagram.

There were various tour options and we decided on the Hong Kong Island Tour. It included a ride on the Peak Tram up to Victoria Peak. The view of the city was beautiful. As the Tram went up the hill, all the building seemed to be at an angle. It was an incredible experience! It's one of the oldest trams in the world and rises about 1,300 feet above sea level.

From there the tour went to Tiger Balm Gardens where there were sculptures and Chinese decorations portraying historical events. We continued on to the "Waikiki of Hongkong" Repulse Bay Beach and then to a fishing village with floating restaurants.

We did a lot of browsing and walking around the shops and I bought a brown suit, it cost $10 American, $100 with Hong Kong money, which I wore out a lot and then shipped home.

Each night my escort and I would go to a night club and dance.
I loved to dance, still do. I was in Hong Kong for a total of five days
looking around, eating pizza, getting a massage and just generally
forgetting that I had to go back to a war zone.

Chapter Twenty-Three — Back from R&R

I arrived at LZ Sally upon my return from R&R and hitched a ride on a log bird to my unit in the field, they were in the foothills. Command said they had an instant NCO, that's a noncommissioned officer, coming out to us. In the states, before he was sent over, he went to special training for 90 days NCO training.

The Lieutenant told me that the NCO was going out with my squad, and he was in charge. We were to go out 500 meters from where the platoon was stationed to set up an ambush site.

I asked one guy in the squad, privately, to keep pace and let me know when we had reached the 500 meters. He was really good at keeping track and so, at the 500 mark he gave me a nod.

I stopped the NCO and asked how far out our destination was. He said 500 meters but when I asked how far we were he couldn't answer. I questioned him about who had kept count, him or if he had assigned it to someone and again, he didn't know. He asked me how far I thought we had traveled, and I told him I knew we were at the 500-meter mark because my counter had kept track.

Safe in the Perimeter of His Hands

I wasn't impressed with this NCO at all.

We began to set up and I let him take charge of it although I didn't have a lot of faith in him succeeding. He didn't know anything about trip flares or how to lay out claymores. I had to explain what they were and show him how to get fortified into a fox hole and put up the firing stakes. We had three defensive fox holes that night and set up our firing stakes to mark the safe range. I told him to call in our marking round, but he didn't know where we were on the map or how to go about calling it in.

It was like I was babysitting, in the middle of a war zone!

I got on the radio and contacted the lieutenant. The RTO and I worked off the map I had, a previous one, and found the point of origin. The lieutenant then moved that to the new map. I told him where we were and set the marking rounds. It was a puff of smoke right above us that lasted just seconds so the enemy wouldn't see it.

It was an uneventful night, which I was thankful for! The next morning, we packed up by rolling up our trip flairs and clay mores. When we arrived back to the platoon and the NCO had to report to the lieutenant, I wanted to be a fly on the wall. I wondered how much he was actually able to report. When the next log bird came in, that NCO

left and we never saw him again. He definitely lacked field

knowledge.

Tom is on the left in the grass

Chapter Twenty-Four — Buck Fever

We were sent out on a three-day mission along a well-used supply trail to set up an ambush site; the North Vietnamese and Viet Cong were moving much needed food and equipment. We were often doing this, setting up an ambush and waiting. It was a boring job, we were on our bellies the whole time, quiet and you couldn't smoke; I didn't but it was hard for those guys who did. It was, however, a great way to catch up on some needed rest. There were so many of us, usually ten or twelve, that you could sleep before it was time for your guard duty again.

Let me explain an ambush site; if the trail runs north to south through the jungle, then we would all be set up on the west side. On the north end would be three guys with clay mores twenty to thirty feet apart, the same on the south and then the rest of the guys in the middle. The kill zone would be consistent for about fifty feet with the mines intersecting each other.

The way it worked was thus: you let the enemy walk through, the first guy is walking through from the north side to the south allowing you to see how many enemies there are. You don't want to blow the clay more on the first guy, you don't know how many are behind waiting to attack you, so you allow the first one to enter and pass you.

So, on this particular ambush we were all set up. There were twelve of us, a squad and then Lieutenant Cody with his RTO. I was the squad leader and positioned in the middle with Cody at the north end. It had been a boring few days of constant sleeping, eating and crawling away to pee, without any enemy activity. It was midday and I was off duty and asleep when I heard a mine go off.

There was instant screaming of pain and Cody started shouting 'I got him, I got him.'. I immediately crawled over to them and saw that the Viet Cong was facing south, meaning he had just walked past the lieutenant, entering the kill zone. I asked how many there were, and Cody just looked at me for a second before his face registered shock; he had killed the first guy who walked through!

The Viet Cong was on the ground, crying and withering in pain. His legs had been blown off from the knees down; there were pieces of material and flesh everywhere, blood streaming from what was left of his legs and his stumps looked like hamburger. I did the humane thing as I walked past him, up the trail.

I shot him in the back of the head.

Several yards down the trail revealed a wet spot with only one set of tracks.

He was alone, probably a messenger of some sort.

I called out to Cody as I was coming back into the ambush site, not wanting to get shot. He still seemed panicked and at the time I thought he had buck fever. I remember deer hunting with my dad on Mt. Scott when I was just eleven, there was an open area and a nice buck was there. My dad told the guy who was with us to go ahead and shoot it, that it was his.

The guy shot, missed the deer and then proceeded to eject all of his shells onto the ground and said, 'did you see that, shot all my rounds and missed him every time'. My dad had said it was buck fever, the guy was so excited that he wasn't sure what was going on.

The lieutenant blew it and he realized it. He later thanked me for not making a big deal out of it and we were close after that. We ended up cleaning up the area, pulling the body into the brush and putting some dirt and brush over it.

A human body would start to decay really fast in the heat, and we were to stay at that location for several more days. We didn't see any more activity; they actually extended our mission two more days, but we never saw another enemy.

We did try out some new trip flairs. They had a sensor that was hooked to the flairs and came back to headphones. They were designed to allow us to hear the enemy approaching but we only ever heard rodents and other creatures. We used these over a span of ten to fifteen days before it was declared that they didn't help, and we went back to the original flairs.

Lilies on a slow-moving stream

Chapter Twenty-Five — It's Not Racism, It's War!

When someone was able to go on R&R, their job would be passed to another person. I was squad leader and an African American kid, who packed a grenade launcher, passed his weapon and vest to another guy. Now the M-70 grenade launcher has shells that are three inches across and six to eight inches long. It would fire a grenade 35-meters and had a kill range of five meters. The round has a spin-activation safety feature that armed itself after it had traveled approximately thirty meters, meaning it had to travel that far in order to explode. The soldier would wear a vest with pockets that hold the grenade shells.

After the exchange, the guy who received the weapon and vest came to me and said that all the shells weren't there; he was only packing half the amount required. I ordered more to be sent in on the next log bird and we went about our business.

When the guy returned from R&R I asked how it went. After hearing all about his adventures, I handed back his vest and told him that all of his rounds were there and that he **would** carry the proper amount.

The guy immediately replied with, "you're only picking on me cause I'm black" and I explained that no, we were all on the same side and we work as a team, together. His orders were to carry x number of shells and he would carry that amount.

End of story.

Things carried on like normal until a typhoon came in and started flooding everything. We were ordered to high ground which was hard to find since we were in rice paddy lands. The winds blew hard, and the rain just kept coming down harder. Before long everything was flooded, the rice paddies, the villages. The water was so high you couldn't tell the rivers from the rice paddies.

But regardless of the weather, the missions went on.

Navy Boat

Our company commander talked to the Navy, and we were issued a boat with oars but no motor. Our platoon, thirty guys, climbed into the boat with the captain. We left our packs behind, they were secured somewhere, and we had day packs. They contained several rounds of ammo.

206

Patrol boat flying a US flag.

The captain really wanted to get some enemy. He figured they would have a hard time getting around with all the water and so we set out looking for them. The water varied in depth from our waists to well over our heads. We were paddling along, everyone on lookout, when we heard what sounded like a mortar going off. Everyone dived over the side of the boat and into the water.

To the onlooker it would have really looked funny, thirty guys in the water and all you could see were the helmets and eye; we probably looked like turtles.

Everyone tenses, waiting for the mortar to land, but it never does.

One guy looked into the boat and saw a grenade shell caught in the seam of the boat. A shell that has been fired from the grenade launcher! It hadn't traveled the required distance to arm itself, so it hadn't gone off. But there it was, live.

The captain looked over at the African American soldier, who was holding the launcher. There is a safety rule when holding the launcher: if you are in combat then there is a shell in it and the launcher is closed. If you aren't in combat, then its broke open. He broke the rule by having it loaded and closed. Some guys are really good with the grenade launcher and can actually get three shells fired and in the air at once.

The captain laid into that guy, called him a stupid idiot, pointing out with several swear words that he could have killed all of us. He talked about the concussion from the boat if that shell had gone off. The captain then ordered everyone away from the boat and had that guy, he was almost white with fear, pick up the shell and toss it away from us into the trees. I walked over to him after that, as everyone was getting back into the boat and said, "you didn't tell him you were black."

Kids with their water buffalo

About a half hour later we were all back in and paddling along when we heard small rifle fire over us. We jumped off, again doing the turtle look. Rounds were landing all around us. We could see mussel flashes and we started shooting back. We had an M60 machine gun with us and started laying down a line of fire.

The captain got on the radio immediately, having the RTO call in artillery. The artillery radios back that there are ARVINs there, the

South Vietnam soldiers.

They were on our side.

We quickly cease fire and the captain got them on the radio. They were such lousy shots they didn't hit any of us, but we wounded two or three of them. We had just been in a fire fight with the friendlies.

A couple days later the water receded enough that we had to return the boat and go back to the normal grunt of walking.

Chapter Twenty-Six —
Tour of Duty Is Up

The third week of February 1969 brought orders on the log bird for me to report to the 1st Sergeant at LZ Sally. I hopped on the helicopter and that afternoon I was standing before the 1st Sergeant. He told me that my tour of duty was about up and if I chose to go state side, I was eligible for an early out of the army.

First though, he said he was authorized to offer me a chance to re-up. He said with my outstanding record I would get a $6000 cash incentive and could stay there and continue in my current position or go home for a month and then come back. Knowing that he made much the same offer to everyone leaving I told him 'Thanks, but No Thanks!'

He did talk me into buying the yearbook of the 101st Airborne Division in Vietnam. That was when he told me that in the last year, the platoon I was in had only two men who went home that hadn't been either wounded or killed. Of course, I wasn't one of them having been wounded in August of 1968.

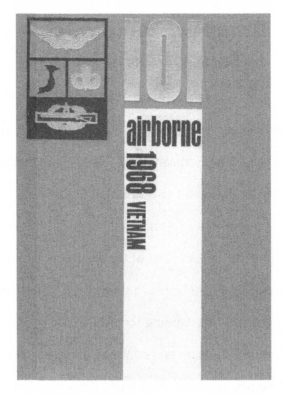

The yearbook

I picked up my duffel bag back from supply that had been stored for a year, got my orders and caught a flight to Bien Hoa. After making my way from the airport to headquarters and getting processed through with more orders, I received ribbons that I wasn't even aware of. Come to find out they keep pretty good records on what each of us did in combat.

I received:

The Combat Infantryman Badge, August 24th, 1968

Air Medal (2)

We would repel from helicopters and ride the skids as they would hoover above the ground for us to jump off. One needed thirty-seven assaults to get an air medal and they issued me two when I left country.

1. Dated January 31st, 1969, and signed by Major General M.Z., Commander, 101st Airborne Division. Awarded for meritorious achievement while participating in aerial flight in the Republic of Vietnam on September 1, 1968.

2. Dated February 9th, 1969, and signed by the same Commander. Awarded the First Oak Leaf Cluster for meritorious achievement while participating in aerial flight in the Republic of Vietnam on January 25th, 1969.

Army Commendation Medal (2)

Bronze Star Medal (5)

The Bronze Star Medal is awarded for meritorious service for each campaign a person has participated in.

I received five having been in the

Tet Counteroffensive (January 30th, 1968 - April 1st 1968);

Vietnam Counteroffensive, Phase IV (April 2nd, 1968- June 30th 1968);

Phase V (July 1st, 1968 – November 1st, 1968);

Vietnam Counteroffensive, Phase VI (November 2nd, 1968-February

22nd, 1969),

Tet 69 Counteroffensive (February 23rd, 1969- June 8th, 1969).

A silver service star is worn instead of five bronze service stars.

Vietnam Service Medal with silver service star

Purple Heart

National Defense Service Medal

Vietnam Defense Service Medal

Vietnam Campaign Medal

Expert Marksmanship Qualification Badge with Rifle Bar
(M-14)

Expert Marksmanship Qualification Badge with Machine
Gun Bar (M-16)

Sharpshooter Marksmanship Qualification Badge with
Rifle Bar (M-16)

Safe in the Perimeter of His Hands

My unit was cited for the **Republic of Vietnam Gallantry Cross with Palm Unit Citation** (April 19th, 1968 – August 15th, 1968) and the **Republic of Vietnam Civil Actions Honor Medal First Class Unit Citation** (March 18th, 1968 – May 2nd, 1970)

I had turned in my combat equipment, rifle, ammo, grenades, and such so it really felt like I would be going home. At headquarters base camp at Bien Hoa, there was another recruiting officer and, to my surprise, also a man, authorized by the Shah of Iran, Mohammad Reza Pahlavi, trying to recruit combat trained and experienced mercenaries to go to Iran. He needed guards for the oil pipelines.

The money was really tempting; one could make more in three months over there than a year at the job I was going back to at the sawmill. I didn't even take their business card; I didn't need the temptation.

After all that I had a night and most of a day to wait for my flight going home. The NCO club was just down the street from the barracks I was to sleep in, so I went over to have a little peace and quiet with a cold refreshment. I sat at the bar and ordered a cold Pepsi, that was a treat after all the hot ones I'd had, when I heard my name.

Safe in the Perimeter of His Hands

I looked around and saw that E7, Walker, who had been in such a hurry to gain his CIB that he killed one and wounded two guys in a neighboring fox hole. The sight of him ruined my day. He came right up to me, clasped me on the shoulder, like we were friends.

I glared at him and said I was surprised to see him here instead of in the stockade for murder. I have to admit there was foul language used. Just with the retelling of this that old rage surfaces some; the ignorance and stupidity, the greed for an accommodation caused three soldiers' pain and death that they didn't even see coming.

I walked back to the barracks after that and had trouble getting to sleep. Sometime in the night we were all awakened by a rocket attack. Someone in charge ran in and told us to go to the armory and pick up a weapon and ammo and take a position on the perimeter of the airfield.

I remember thinking, 'after a year of combat, where I could have been killed so often, let's get through one more night'. Finally, just before day light we were told to stand down, turn in our weapons and find our bunks.

I did get a shower (what a treat!) that morning!

It was midafternoon when we were finally told to line up, the plane was about to land. I watched a line of young men, boys really, clean and rested, march off that flight and couldn't help wondering how many of them would make it home next year.

I remembered walking off that flight after a twenty-seven-hour flight in which I had nothing to do other than eat and sleep. Now I stand here, a year later with never enough to eat, twenty pounds lighter and not one full night of sleep; no wonder we look the way we do coming and going.

Vietnamese Greyhound

Chapter Twenty-Seven — Home

On the plane we ate and slept for the twenty-seven-hour flight. It was just getting dark out when the captain of the aircraft spoke over the intercom and said 'We have just entered the airspace of the Continental United States of America. Those lights you see out your window are San Francisco'.

Emotions hit me like a freight train: joy, peace, and excitement. It felt like a weight I had been living with lifted from my shoulders.

I made it home!

I felt a tear drop onto my hand and it jarred me back to where I was. Looking around the plane, full of battle-weary soldiers, there wasn't a dry eye on board.

We were home.

We had been sent to hell and made it out alive and back home.

I really did make it back!

But why did I survive? When so many had fallen beside me, why me?

It was a question I would continue to ponder on for years.

On the plane I found a typed letter in my things; it was made

218

Safe in the Perimeter of His Hands

by the 101st Airborne and says this:

"Dear Civilians, Friends, Draft Dodgers, etc.

In the very near future, the undersigned will once more be in your midst, dehydrated and demoralized, to take his place again as a human being with the well-known forms of freedom and justice for all; engage in life, liberty and the somewhat delayed pursuit of Happiness. In making your joyous preparations to welcome him back into organized society you might take certain steps to make allowances for the crude environment which has been his miserable lot for the past twelve months. In other words, he might be a little Asiatic from Vietnamese itis and overseasitis, all should be handled with care. Do not be alarmed if he is infected with all forms of rare tropical diseases. A little time in the "Land of the Big PX" will cure his malady.

Therefore, show no alarm if he insists on carrying a weapon to the dinner table, looks around for his steel pot when offered a chair, or wakes you up in the middle of the night for guard duty. Keep cool when he pours gravy on his dessert at dinner of mixes peaches with his Seagram's VO. Pretend not to notice if he eats with his fingers instead of silverware and prefers C-Rations to steak. Take it with a smile when he insists on digging up the garden to fill sandbags for the bunker he is building. Be tolerant when he takes his blanket and sheet off the bed and puts them on the floor to sleep on.

Abstain from saying anything about powdered eggs, dehydrated potatoes, fried rice, fresh milk or ice cream. Do not be alarmed if he should jump up from the dinner table and rushes to the garbage can to wash his dish with a toilet brush. After all this has been his standard. Also, if it should start raining pay no attention to him if he pulls off his clothes, grabs a bar of soap and towel and runs outdoors for a shower.

When in his daily conversation he utters such things as Sin Loi, and Choi Oi, just be patient and leave quickly and calmly if by some chance he utters 'Didi' with an irritated look on his face, because it means no less than "get the hell out of here". Do not let it shake you up if he picks up the phone and yells Airborne Sir or says Roger Out for goodbye, or simply shouts "short".

Never ask why the Jones's son held a higher rank than he did and by no means mention the term 'extended'. Pretend not to notice if at a restaurant he calls the waitress 'number one girls' and uses his hat for an ashtray. He will probably keep listening for 'Coming Home Soldier' to sound off over AFRS. If he does, comfort him for he is reminiscing. Be especially watchful when he is in the presence of a women...especially a beautiful woman.

Above all, keep in mind that beneath that tanned and rugged exterior that is a heart of gold (the only think of value he has left). Treat him with kindness, tolerance, and an occasional 5th of good liquor, and you will be able to rehabilitate the happy go lucky guy you once knew and loved.

Last, but not by no means least, send no more mail to the APO, fill the ice box with beer, get the civvies out of the mothballs, fill the car with gas and get the women and children off the street....
BECAUSE THIS KID IS COMING HOME!

Signature: "

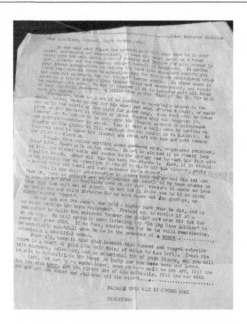

In twenty-four hours, I had gone through the Army discharge process. It really wasn't much of a process. I received a steak dinner, any outstanding pay; I made $90 a month. Finishing with a twenty-minute physical and the issuing of a new uniform, which I was advised not to wear home as the public wasn't very friendly to GI's.

So, with no debriefing, no evaluation from doctors on mental fitness, I walked away from the Army and bought a bus ticket from Oakland, California to Roseburg, Oregon. I had worn my uniform, maybe it was just pride; that I survived, that I was home. I'm not sure what I was thinking at the time, but I found out very quickly that they were right in their advisement.

The GI was an enemy at home.

People threw feces, spit at us, called us baby killers and other crude names. Instead of a wave, it was the middle finger.

There wasn't a welcome like I had heard about with the WWII veterans. No parade, no welcoming signs. The Vietnam war went from 1964 to 1973, the longest running war at that time and in the American eye, it was a lost war. The veteran was made to feel ashamed and guilty; unwanted.

Tom Barrett, a Vietnam memorial committee chairman said it best, "It's never too long for these people to be recognized. These people weren't recognized 40 years ago. These people didn't choose the war they fought in. These people just stood up and did their duty and accepted the ultimate fate."

I arrived home to Glide, Oregon, with very little fanfare. I remember my younger brother, Mike, asking to see my ribbons and metals. When I pulled them out my father, who had served in the Navy but never saw combat, without even looking away from the television, said 'They were just handing them out over there'. I put all my medals away and didn't pull them out again.

One day the yearbook I had purchased arrived, and I was surprised to see people I knew and the places I'd been. There's even a picture of me helping with a big rice cache, loading it into nets for a chinook helicopter.

The rice cache

I'm on the left, moving bags of rice

Weapons cache

Major General O.M. Barsanti, Commander of 101st Airborne

Division, wrote "You came with a job to do-defeat the enemy-and you

226

have done this job well. To accomplish this, we have employed every resource in the command, day and night. My philosophy is simple: continuous attack with multiple actions; always attack under an umbrella of friendly artillery; when a lucrative target is found, mass forces; and company size actions continuous around the clock on all fronts. You are experts at the art of night fighting and jungle fighting; you have learned well the valuable lesson of reacting violently to enemy fire, never break contact and shoot low. You are a well decorated, distinguished unit…you have established records that other units have not surpassed in much longer periods of time." Excerpt from the *101 Airborne 1968 Vietnam Yearbook.*

Chapter Twenty-Eight — Getting Back to Living

Nothing was the same.

I wasn't the same.

A car could backfire, and I would be on the sidewalk, usually grabbing whoever was with me and hauling them down also.

I didn't hunt; that pastime I had so loved as a young teen was destroyed as a soldier. I had done my share of hunting and killing, and it held no enjoyment for me.

I went back to work at the sawmill and shortly after started being harassed by a cop. I would be pulled over most days after leaving the sawmill. He would ask for my identification and glance inside my truck before letting me go. This happened six times within a two-month period. Finally, when he asked for my identification, I told him that he knew who I was, that he had pulled me over 5 times previously and I wanted to know why.

He finally admitted that he wasn't supposed to tell me this, but the Chief of Police and the DA had given instructions to pull over any Vietnam veterans because they were suspected of receiving pot from

Vietnam and selling it. Him and I had a very frank talk after that, and he didn't pull me over again.

I went through my days surviving after that but not really living.

I didn't start living until I met Keith Smith.

Keith and Jeanette Smith

I knew Keith, he was our neighbor and I had attended school with his kids, but I hadn't really spent time with him. Keith invited me to church one Sunday and it was there that I learned about love.

My family didn't believe in God; my father believed he could do it all and my mother flirted with the Jehovah Witness religion for a while, but I think it was more of a social thing. I know I was loved as a child; I was the oldest of 6 children, but there was no comparing the love I felt in that small Church of Christ.

The hymns, the message, the warm hugs.

It was addicting.

I started attending regularly and in June of 1971, I gave my life to Christ. It was one of the happiest days of my life.

February 17, 1978, was another happy day.

Tom and Jennifer

Jennifer Smith, Keith's daughter, and I were married and in the next six years we had four kids: Alicia, Daniel, Daisy and Allison.

North Family
Top – Alicia
2ⁿᵈ row – Daniel and Tom
3ʳᵈ row – Daisy and Jennifer
Bottom – Allison

Jennifer has a Batchelor's of Science degree from Oregon State University. She helped pay off her parent's ranch and took over running it shortly after she graduated, raising hogs and sheep. We continued and added beef and logging to the mix along with our four kids.

Tom taking a break from logging

When Allison, our youngest, was about 5, Jennifer broached the subject of camping. I scoffed at that notion and quickly told her I had done all my camping in Vietnam. It wasn't something I was ever going to do again. She informed me that the kids hadn't been camping and it was selfish of me to have that attitude. So, she wrote out the lists and filled the packs while I decided where to go.

Twin Lakes was a place I knew well from my youth, the big lake is fourteen acres and the little one is six acres. It is located between the North Umpqua River and Little River and can be reached from either side. The North Umpqua side is a fairly smooth walk and is about a three-and-a-half-mile hike in. The Little River side, however, is a straight up the hill seven-mile hike. I didn't even hesitate when I decided; we were walking in from the Little River side and I wouldn't have to do this camping thing again. One trip would do them in.

Wow, how I underestimated my family! They loved it!

It quickly became our main vacation, high mountain lake camping. We didn't pack tents but instead everyone camped in the open, in sleeping bags, on a tarp.

Tom and Jennifer on a camping trip

Jennifer cooked over the open fire and delivered amazing meals that were gobbled up by the four. Since then, we have been to Twin Lakes many times, from the North Umpqua side (I got in big trouble when they found out there was an easier route).

After that first time, we would look up lakes and plan our excursions. We've been to several, including Maidu, which is the over the Pacific Crest Trail and the headwaters of the Umpqua River; it's about a four-and-a-half-mile walk.

Miller Lake, a natural freshwater lake, is in western Klamath County and is the trailhead for Maidu. One trip, we decided to drive there and camp. We set up two tents and the kids went about playing. That night it froze, you could see a slight sheen of ice across the lake and the water we had left in cups and pans was frozen solid.

We walked into Skookum, seeing small pikas along the way and found the ground covered by little black toads. Cliff Lake was beautiful, sitting below two massive peaks, but held no fish.

We drove to Summit Lake and pitched a tent, thankfully. Shortly after setting up, a storm moved in with lightning flashing across the lake and rain pouring down like sheets. Daniel rushed out and dug a trench around the tent so we wouldn't float away.

A short drive up the North Umpqua was Toketee. We would load up the truck, all the kids, their friends and the dogs and head up for the day or the weekend.

Camping
Top – Jennifer and Daisy
Middle Row – Friend, Allison, Alicia, Friend, Friend
Bottom Row – Tom, Friend, Friend holding grandson Timothy, Friend

But beyond the camping, Jennifer and I chose to be present with our children and worked either on the ranch or self-employed doing custom haying, backhoe work, delivering rock and cleaning

235

culverts. The kids were able to go with us or stay on the ranch with Jennifer's mom.

Tom is in the back on the left, feeding a calf in demonstration to an elementary class.

We immersed ourselves in the church with me becoming an elder, Jennifer teaching and eventually both of us becoming youth leaders. We took two different trips to Mexico to build houses. I would go to the house site and help, and Jennifer would stay at camp and cook all the meals.

236

Mexico mission trip 1995;
the homeowner was proud of this gun
and wanted us to see it.

Mexico Mission Trip; Alicia and Daniel mixing cement for the stucco finish.

Disneyland 1995; every mission trip ended with a trip to Disneyland. Jennifer and Tom.

Thanksgiving and Spring Breaks we packed up the kids and Jennifer's mom and headed to California to visit Aunt Babe. She was Jennifer's aunt and lived North of Leggett at the World-Famous Tree House where she worked; Jennifer had spent summers working there in her youth.

The kids loved it. Babe would get us a room not far from the tree and we would invade her space for a few days, playing in the redwoods, going to the beach, and just enjoying family time.

World-Famous Tree House.
Back row – Babe holding Allison, Tom, Jennifer
Alicia is to the left then Daniel and Daisy

As the children grew older and eventually started to marry, they gave us grandchildren, a real joy to aging parents; we now have nine.

Jennifer and Tom

Alicia, our first born, is married to Russel. They have two sons, Connor and Quinn. Alicia has a degree in Equine Science and a Batchelor's of Science in Criminal Justice. Russel was in the Marines for four years, serving in Iraq. He has a master's degree in teaching and is a high school math teacher. They have a small farm close by with horses and raise honeybees and goats. Connor and Quinn are very active boys and are involved with 4-H, baseball and wrestling, where they have placed high in every match they've done. We are so proud of them!

Alicia, Russel
Conner, Quinn

Our son, Daniel, is the second born. He has a degree in viticulture and helps runs the ranch; he is currently raising buffalo and is working on opening part of the ranch for campers. He works at a local sawmill as a sawyer. He has two children, Timothy and Olivia. Timothy is currently serving in the Airforce and is stationed in Europe.

Olivia is a recent high school graduate and is working at the sawmill. She has a great love for animals and a talent for photography. We can't wait to see what the future holds for both of them.

Timothy, Olivia, Daniel

Daisy is our third child and is married to Tim. They have two kids, Emma and Noah. Daisy was a CNA and then a Licensed Massage Therapist for ten years before making a career change and becoming a sales assistant at a television station. Tim has been in the grocery business his whole life and is now a store manager. Emma was born on our anniversary, and we tell her all the time that she is the best anniversary gift ever. She is a talented dancer and has been in several plays. Noah is an excellent pianist and they both enjoy playing soccer and are excellent students.

Daisy, Tim
Noah, Emma

My last, but not least, is Allison. She is married to Jim, and they have three amazing little girls, Sabrina, Sanora and Sofia. Allison was an account manager for Coca-Cola for several years but wanted to spend more time with her family and chose to move in with us, a real blessing at our age, and now works at the girl's school. Jim works for

243

the same grocery store as Tim, only in a different town. The girls are very active and love the outdoors, animals, and going to dance and church. It's very special having them live with us and seeing them grow up.

Jim, Sofia, Allison
Sabrina, Sanora

We are very proud of all of our kids and grandkids. Each and every one is special and a true blessing to our lives.

Tom is now the chaplain at VWF Post 2468

Tom and Jennifer, 2021, Sisters Oregon

Tom 2019, showing how to ride on a skid.

Chapter Twenty-nine — The Why

I'm so thankful, looking back, that God guided me in those critical moments of deciding life and death during the war. I know He was with me, even though I wasn't with Him.

All through the years I wondered and sometimes verbally asked why God had brought me home, why did I live, and others die?

What was the reason?

May of 2011 marked my 64th birthday, over 42 years being home from Vietnam. In June of 2011 Allison, who was the last to be married, was doing just that (Alicia, our oldest was in the hospital having her youngest son, Quinn!).

The wedding day will be remembered by all. The setting was beautiful: a green lawn overlooking the setting sun on the Pacific Ocean, a catered dinner, a large dance floor and the DJ with all the handpicked songs.

Like all weddings there were a few hiccups – it rained all day (and only that day), the beautiful cake which the bride somehow found time to make in all this, fell over and a seagull pooped on the lapel of my tux. But, as all good stories with happy endings, the ceremony was moved inside, Jennifer and Daisy did some kind of miracle on the cake, putting the pieces back together and my lapel was wiped clean with no one the wiser.

Jim, Allison, Jennifer and Tom

After the ceremony they were doing the things you do at weddings, cut the cake, toast, dinner, then the dances: parents of the bride, parents of the groom, then the father and bride. She had the DJ play an old song, Daddies Girl, and it was lovely with just Allison and myself out on the dance floor talking about how well it all went, and I told her how nice she looked and how proud I was of her.

Allison and I

Then she put her cheek against mine and I could feel the tears when she told me, "You know how you always wondered why God let you come home from Vietnam? He knew you would be a great dad! I'm so glad we're here together because you are the best of Dads."

There it was.

Forty-two years of waiting and it was Allison's voice and from her heart, but it was God speaking to me. Even though I didn't come to know Him till after Vietnam, He knew me.

He held me in the safe perimeter of His hands for that year and since.

I am so blessed!

My Beautiful Family

Unit History

This is the day-to-day history of the time I was in Vietnam.

We have kept in the beginning of the year, 1968, just to give the history of where the unit was stationed. For ease of reading, we have made the dates flow month then day and have expanded the military abbreviations (except for the ones we didn't know).

The Battalion was broke into four companies, Alpha (A), Bravo (B) Charlie (C) and Delta (D). This history varies on what is used: the term or letter. I was in Bravo, B Company.

This is the unit history for the 1st Battalion, 502d Airborne Infantry, for the year 1968.

For the commander: Earl C. Jackson, Jr. First Lieutenant, Infantry

PREFACE:
This annual supplement to the unit history of the 1st Battalion, 502d Infantry in a brief narrative description of the unit's activities during combat operations in Vietnam which took place throughout the calendar year.

The Battalion was just beginning contact operations in Vietnam on January 1st. The Battalion arrived in Vietnam during December 1967. After the Battalion arrived at Bien Hoa, on December 15th, 1967, it moved to Chu Chi, Vietnam, where the Battalion was located at the start of this reporting period.

The Battalion had made four separate contacts with the enemy during December 1967, resulting in 6 friendly wounded, by hostile actions and 3 killed by hostile action. The Battalion killed 4 enemy by body count in those engagements.

WILSON GAROLD THOMAS	SFC	30	24-Oct-67	B CO
BINKO GEORGE	PFC	21	27-Dec-67	A CO
CASON WILLIAM ARNOLD	PFC	21	27-Dec-67	A CO

The Battalion has numerous news articles and photographs on file at the Battalion which compliment this narrative description of the Battalion's activities.

NARRATIVE:

The Battalion conducted training and maintenance at the garrison in Chu Chi for preparation of future contact operations on January 1st and 2nd.

SUPPLEMENT HISTORY FOR CALENDAR YEAR 1968.

As 1968 opened, Headquarters and Headquarters Company was located at Chu Chi, Republic of Vietnam. Commanding was Captain Terrance Neil Spiegelberg. The calendar year 1968 presented the Company with logistical and administrative problems, in support of the numerous operations conducted by the Second Brigade. Significant personnel turbulence was experienced during the year. Most of this was due to the big "DEROS Hump" (Date of Expected Return from Overseas) in November. The Security Platoon conducted patrols at Chu Chi with very little contact.

From January 22nd to 29th, the Company moved from Chu Chi to Phu Bai Airfield. This move was conducted by Air Force C-130 aircraft. The Brigade began operation, "Jeb Stuart". During this time, we received logistical support from Fire Support Area Mac Donald, located at Landing Zone El Paso (now Camp Eagle). Re-supply was accomplished by vehicles, and adequacy depended on road conditions and clearance.

On January 27th the Company moved to Landing Zone El Paso by road convoy. This greatly reduced many of our logistical problems.

Landing Zone El Paso come under 60mm mortar fire the morning of January 31ˢᵗ. Bravo Company 326 Medical Battalion reported 4 killed in the action and 4 wounded in the action. Counter mortar fire engaged the enemy position with unknown results.

February saw the Brigade in the middle of operation, "Jeb Stuart". Many logistical problems occurred under the constant moving concept used by the Brigade. There was a great shortage of TA 50-901 (standard issue of combat clothing and equipment), clothing, batteries, Logistics Support Area (a depot or hub with supplies), all types of class IV barrier material (construction, fortification and barrier materials), demolitions, hand grenades, trip flares, booby traps, and claymore mines.

First Log command was unable to provide shower, laundry service, potable water, and graves registration section. The lack of these services created severe health and sanitation problems.

In February 1968, Captain James P. Downey assumed command. The security Platoon operated between Landing Zone El Paso and Landing Zone Jane. They participated in the securing of QL#1 (Highway One, the main road from Ho Chi Minh City to Hanoi).

In March the whole Brigade Headquarters moved to Landing Zone Sally. This would be the final move by the Brigade in 1968.

On March 10ᵗʰ, operation "Jeb Stuart" came to a close.

Many lessons were learned during the very successful operation. Valuable lessons that would be put to use in later operations.

On March 10ᵗʰ, operation "Carentan I" started. Treatment, evacuation and hospitalization of casualties was accomplished by the 571st

Medical Detachment to Company B, 326 Medical Battalion. For more serious injuries, the patients were sent to 22nd Surgical Hospital, located at Phu Bai. The decision is made there to further evacuate the injured personnel to Japan, or the USA.

DAILY ACCOUNT:

Jan 3rd - Battalion conducted combat assault. 1st lift airborne 08:07 hours, last lift completed 09:17 hours.

Bravo and Alpha discovered numerous booby traps and fresh sign. Delta made heavy contact. Battalion set up for night in company night defense positions. All night defense positions were mortared during the night.

Casualties: (slight) 23 wounded in action; 13 wounded in action and evacuated.

Results to date:

Friendly: 19 wounded in action, 1 killed in action

Enemy: 10 North Vietnamese Army battle casualties

January 4th - During early morning hours, the Night Defense Positions of A & D received rockets in their perimeter. During daylight hours Battalion conducted search and destroy operations. Charlie made heavy contact and was supported by gunships and artillery. Charlie had 10 wounded in action. Bravo moved to support Charlie and came under heavy contact with 7 killed in action and 1 wounded in action. One man discovered mission in action.

Results to date:

Friendly - 36 wounded in action, 1missing in action, 8 killed in action.

Enemy: - 27 killed in action as battle casualty; 2 wounded in action taken as prisoner of war

KELMAN, WAYNE H.	CPL	21	04-Jan-68	C CO
LONG, RICHARD LYTLE	SSG	23	04-Jan-68	C CO
MC CRAY, THOMAS	CPL	29	04-Jan-68	C CO
ROY, JAMES WILLIE, 3RD	SP4	20	04-Jan-68	C CO
SIMON, DAVID LOWELL	SSG	19	04-Jan-68	C CO
SWEET, EUGENE FREDERICK JR;	PFC	18	04-Jan-68	C CO
WISHAM, GEORGE MERRITT JR	2LT	23	04-Jan-68	C CO
GABRIEL, MEREDITH ALTON	SGT	20	04-Jan-68	HHC

Jan 5th - Battalion continued search and destroy missions around Cu Chi.
Bravo linked up with a tank unit and returned to area of contact to find missing in action. Body found and identified as missing man. Other companies had negative contact and returned to Cu Chi for night.
Change: 1 missing in action to 1 killed in action

Jan 6th - Battalion continued training and remained in perimeter of Cu Chi. During the night hours movement heard around perimeter. At 21:30 hours a light was shined on a bunker and a sniper shot one man Results: 1 wounded in action

Jan 7th - Battalion conducted heli-borne lift to landing zone X-Ray and set up for night.

Jan 8th - Battalion conducted search and destroy mission vicinity of landing zone X-Ray. No contact made.

Jan 10th - Battalion conducted movement back to and closed on Cu Chi. No contact.

Jan 11th -14th - Battalion conducted training in preparation for upcoming operations.

Jan 14th - Battalion heli-lifted to landing zone Gold. Choppers received ground fire, but no contact was made. Perimeter formed.

Jan 15th - Battalion conducted search and destroy mission from landing zone Gold. Scattered very light contact made. Negative results.

Jan 16th - During the early morning hours, Alpha Company ambushed on river, fired on sampan boat.
Results: 4 North Vietnamese Army killed in action, battle casualties. Battalion formed into night defense positions for the night.
Results to date:
Friendly: 37 wounded in action, 9 killed in action
Enemy: 5 wounded in action and taken as prisoner of war, 31 killed in action as battle casualty.

Jan 17th - Battalion continued with search and destroy mission. Light contact during time period. A bunker and tunnel complex was found and destroyed.
Results:
Enemy: 1 Viet Cong killed in action, battle casualty. 8 AK - 47 captured

Jan 18th - Flame throwers were used on tunnels as Battalion continued its search and destroy operations.

Jan 19th - Battalion returned to Cu Chi and had light contact during the period.
Results: 5 wounded in action
Results to date:
Friendly: 42 wounded in action, 9 killed in action
Enemy: 5 wounded in action and taken as prisoner of war, 32 killed in action as battle casualty.

GERWATOWSKI, JOSEPH   SGT   20   19-Jan-68   A CO
MOORE, JAMES RUSSELL   PFC   23   19-Jan-68   A CO

Jan 20th to Feb 4th - Battalion conducted recon in force operations in new area of operation with light contact.

Results:

1 wounded in action and captured, 1 AK-47 captured.

BROWN, JOHN THOMAS   PFC 19 01-Feb-68 A CO
HAMILTON, JAMES EDWARD   SGT 19 01-Feb-68 A CO
HOLLAND, JOSEPH PHILLIP   CPT 25 01-Feb-68 A CO
WITTLER, LARRY ELDON   PVT 19 01-Feb-68 D CO

Feb 5th - During the early morning hours the night perimeter defense of Alpha was heavily engaged by a reinforced North Vietnamese Army company. Heavy contact from 03:26 hours till 09:30 hours when enemy broke contact. Patrols were sent out to assess the situation. Contact made with estimated North Vietnamese Army platoon, 5 North Vietnamese Army killed in action as battle casualty. Company sized sweeps sent out resulting in heavy contact and 20 more North Vietnamese Army killed in action as battle casualty. Alpha and Bravo extracted. Delta made negative contact.

Battalion set up night perimeter defense around Quang Tri for the night.

Results:

Friendly: 33 wounded in action, 1 killed in action

Enemy: 0 wounded in action, 25 killed in action as battle casualty, 100 killed in action (estimated)

Captured: 2 machine guns, 2 AK-47, 1-82mm and 1-60mm Mortar.

MEANS, RONALD LEROY SP4   19   05-Feb-68   B CO

Feb 6th - Battalion continued search and destroy operations southeast of Quang Tri. Very light contact with negative results.

Feb 7th - Battalion continued search and destroy operations south east of Qunag Tri with scattered heavy contact throughout the day. Delta reinforced by Recon and Bravo made contact with estimated North Vietnamese Army reinforced companies.
Results:
Friendly: 6 wounded in action and 2 killed in action.
Enemy: 25 North Vietnamese Army killed in action as battle casualty.
Companies moved to night defense position by dark.
Estimated 100-150 North Vietnamese Army killed in action during the day.

BROWN, RAYMOND   **SP4**   **20**   **07-Feb-68**   **D CO**
URDIALES, ALFRED JR   **PFC**   **18**   **07-Feb-68**   **E CO**

Feb 8th - Battalion continued search and destroy operations southeast of Quan Tri. Light contact was made during the day. Received message from brigade "Aerial observation and other sources gave 1/502 credit for 250 North Vietnamese Army killed in action as battle casualties for period Feb 4th-8th 1968
Results:
Friendly: 82 wounded in action, 12 killed in action
Enemy: 6 wounded in action and taken as prisoners of war, 305 killed in action as battle casualties, 100 killed in action (estimated)
During the night, Alpha and Bravo night defense position were infiltrated by sappers. Attacks very heavy.
Casualties: 8 killed in action, 19 wounded in action, 11 North Vietnamese Army killed in action as battle casualty.

DE MELLO, CLYDE LAWRENCE   **CPL**   **18**   **09-Feb-68**   **A CO**
NORTON, THOMAS   **SP4**   **20**   **09-Feb-68**   **A CO**
NOVEL, CHARLES EDWARD   **SP4**   **21**   **09-Feb-68**   **A CO**
ROUNSEVILLE, JOSEPH WILFRED   **1SG**   **30**   **09-Feb-68**   **A CO**
TEREJKO, BENJAMIN JOHN JR   **SP4**   **20**   **09-Feb-68**   **A CO**
WAITE, DONALD STEVEN   **SP4**   **19**   **09-Feb-68**   **A CO**

CRAWFORD CHARLES J JR   **SP6   20   09-Feb-68   HHC**

Feb 12th - Battalion continues search and destroy operations east of Quang Tri and security landing zone Jane. Contact light with 1 wounded in action by booby-trap.

Feb 13th - Battalion continues search and destroy operations southeast of Quang Tri and security of landing zone Jane. Negative contact made.

Feb 14th - During the reporting period the battalion continued search and destroy operations to the southeast of Quang Tri and continued to furnish security along QL #10 northwest to Hai Lang.

Feb 15th - Battalion continues search and destroy operations with moderate contact made. Combat assault by Bravo received small arms fire during 2nd lift. Negative contact made after that. Alpha and Charlie made contact while sweeping.
Results: 1 wounded in action
Enemy: 14 killed in action

Feb 16th - Battalion continued search and destroy operations with 2 combat assaults by Alpha and Charlie. Heavy contact.
Results:
Friendly: 1 killed in action, 13 wounded in action, 1 missing in action.
Enemy: 18 killed in action as battle casualty.
Results to date:
Friendly: 116 wounded in action, 1 missing in action, 21 killed in action.
Enemy: 6 wounded in action and taken as prisoner of war, 348 killed in action as battle casualty, 100 killed in action (estimated).
SAUNDERS, RANDALL LEROY   **SP4   20   16-Feb-68   A CO**
VOLLMER, VALENTINE BERNARD   **SP4   20   16-Feb-68   A CO**

Feb 17th - Battalion continues search and destroy operations southeast of Quang Tri and conducted one combat assault with Alfa company into the same area as contact of yesterday.
Heavy contact resulted in 1 killed in action and 11 wounded in action with negative enemy assessment.

PERSHING, RICHARD WARREN	**2LT**	**25**	**17-Feb-68**	**A CO**
GREGORY, HENRY	**PFC**	**20**	**17-Feb-68**	**B CO**
HOGE, FRANK LEE	**PFC**	**20**	**17-Feb-68**	**B CO**

Feb 18th - Battalion continues search and destroy operations southeast of Quang Tri with light contact and negative results.

Feb 19th -Battalion continues search and destroy operations with mission of security of QL #1 in area of operation. During this time period 3 Viet Cong killed in action as battle casualty by ambush and 1 US wounded in action later killed in action by mine on QL #1.

HARRELL, RONNIE PFC 19 19-Feb-68 A CO

Feb 20th -Battalion continued with search and destroy and security mission. Light contact during the day with 1 North Vietnamese Army killed in action as battle casualty by ambush.

Feb 21st - Battalion continued with operations and had scattered light to moderate contact by Bravo.
Results:
Friendly: 1 killed in action, 1 wounded in action
Enemy: 4 North Vietnamese Army killed in action as battle casualty.

CANTU, FLORENTINO JR SP4 19 21-Feb-68 B CO

Feb 22nd - Battalion continued search and destroy operations and security QL #1 southeast of Quang Tri. Operations by Alfa resulted in 2 killed in action by grenade attack during security of landing zone Jane. Bravo, while sweeping, made heavy contact. Charlie was ambushed while moving to Bravo's aid. Delta also in heavy contact during the day.

Results:
Friendly: 5 killed in action, 32 wounded in action
Enemy: 12 North Vietnamese Army killed in action as battle casualty.
Estimated North Vietnamese Army battalion in area.

MC GEE, HERMAN	**PFC**	**21**	**22-Feb-68**	**A CO**
NEILL, JOE MELVIN	**PFC**	**18**	**22-Feb-68**	**A CO**
ZAMORA, EDWARD	**SP4**	**20**	**22-Feb-68**	**C CO**
COMBS, JAMES STEPHEN	**SP4**	**19**	**22-Feb-68**	**D CO**
LEVESQUE, ROLAND PHILLIP	**SGT**	**21**	**22-Feb-68**	**D CO**

Feb 23rd - Search and destroy operations continued with security of QL #1. Scattered light contact made with 2 wounded in action by booby trap.
LEHR, DAVID RICHARD   PVT   19   23-Feb-68   D CO

Feb 24th - Search and destroy operations continued with security of QL #1.

Feb 25th -Provided security of QL #1 and bridge (460400) in preparation for Feb 26th operation.

Feb 26th - Battalion cleared and secured assigned section of QL #1 and conducted combat assault with 3 companies. During the period, light combat was experienced, and Alfa's night defense position was probed by sappers.
Results:
Friendly: 2 killed in action, 2 wounded in action
Enemy: 7 North Vietnamese Army killed in action as battle casualty.
KROMREY DENNIS JOHN   PFC   21   26-Feb-68   A CO

Feb 27th - Continued search and destroy operation southeast of Quang Tri and cleared and secured Q.L.#1. Two combat assaults resulted in heavy contact by Bravo and light contact by Charlie.

Results:
Friendly: 12 wounded in action
Enemy: 2 North Vietnamese Army killed in action by battle casualty.
TROLLINGER, JIMMY MICHAEL   PFC   20   27-Feb-68   A CO

Feb 28th - Battalion moved to fire support base Nora, 14 kilometers northwest of Hue, and began operation in new area of operations and Charlie occupied position for preparation of landing zone Sally.

Feb 29th - Began search and destroy operations in new area of operations. Alpha and Delta moved northwest from An Lo bridge. Alpha was taken under fire by estimated company of North Vietnamese Army. Alpha pulled back and called for and received air strikes, artillery, and gunships.
Results: 5 North Vietnamese Army killed in action as battle casualty.
Results to date:
Friendly: 1 missing in action, 177 wounded in action, 31 killed in action.
Enemy: 6 wounded in action and taken as prisoner of war, 377 killed in action as battle casualty, 100 killed in action (estimated).

Mar 1st - Battalion began operations in Quang Tri district from fire support base Nora, An Lo Bridge and continued construction of fire support base Sally. Alpha moved to Ap Lai Xa (YD 638310) where they had made heavy contact on Feb 29th 1968. They found no enemy, but villagers stated that there had been approximately 200 North Vietnamese Army/Vietcong in the village and that they had been up most of the night dragging off their dead. Delta made light contact in vicinity YD 642298 and Battalion company's command and control helicopter was used to kill 126 North Vietnamese Army.
Results: 16 North Vietnamese Army killed in action as battle casualties by Strike's command and control helicopter.

Mar 2nd -Battalion continued search and destroy operations and made light contact throughout the day. Boobytraps caused 3 wounded in action.

Mar 3rd - Battalion continued search and destroy operations from An LO Bridge to (YD 671311) Ap Duc Trong. Bravo and Charlie made heavy contact from village and called for all available fire support and pulled back. After heavy contact for 4 hours, B&C were withdrawn by air. During extraction battalion commanders command and control helicopter received heavy fire, wounding battalion commanding officer, his radio telephone operator, battalion S-2, and command pilot. Battalion S-2, dead on arrival at Evans.
Results:
Friendly: 17 wounded in action, 4 killed in action
Enemy: 1 wounded in action and taken as prisoner of war, 13 killed in action as battle casualty, 48 killed in action (estimated).

BORGMAN, RICHARD LEE	**PFC**	**21**	**03-Mar-68**	**B CO**
FAWKS, ERNEST EUGENE	**SP4**	**30**	**03-Mar-68**	**C CO**
NORFLEET, HENRY JR	**CPL**	**18**	**03-Mar-68**	**C CO**
WILLIAMS, JAMES EARL	**CPL**	**20**	**03-Mar-68**	**C CO**
DIMMITT, FRANK ROBERT	**CPT**	**30**	**03-Mar-68**	**HHC**

Mar 4th - Battalion continued search and destroy operations and conducted joint sweep with Popular Forces in vicinity of An Lo Bridge.
Results: 2 North Vietnamese Army killed in action as battle casualty. Recon made light contact and had 2 men wounded in action.

Mar 5th - Battalion continued search and destroy operations with light contact. 1 man wounded in action from punji pit.

Mar 6th - Heavy contact made by Delta company at 13:43 hours in vicinity of YD698304 (W-Shaped village). Delta broke contact at

16:12 hours and were extracted from the hot landing zone after using all available fire support on village. Estimated 2 reinforced companies in the village.

Results:

Friendly: 5 killed in action, 25 wounded in action, 2 missing in action.

Enemy: 58 killed in action as battle casualty, confirmed by aerial observation

CARPENTER, CLINTON R JR	**SP4**	**21**	**06-Mar-68**	**D CO**
CARR, ALVIN	**PFC**	**19**	**06-Mar-68**	**D CO**
LATRAILLE, DAVID JOHN	**SP4**	**20**	**06-Mar-68**	**D CO**
PALAZZOLA, STEPHEN FRANK	**PFC**	**19**	**06-Mar-68**	**D CO**
PIGFORD, PHILLIP WAYNE	**SGT**	**21**	**06-Mar-68**	**D CO**
SHAMBAUGH, GREGORY RANDALL	**CPL**	**20**	**06-Mar-68**	**D CO**
STYS, STANLEY ALBERT	**PFC**	**18**	**06-Mar-68**	**D CO**

March 7th - Battalion continued search and destroy operations and made 3 company size combat assaults resulting in moderate contact. Bravo recovered the bodies of the 2 missing in action from Delta.

Results:

Friendly: 1 killed in action, 1 wounded in action, 2 missing in action (moved to killed in action)

Enemy: 30 killed in action as battle casualty

TEDRICK, WARREN GAMBIEL JR SGT 20 07-Mar-68 A CO

March 8th - Battalion continued operations and Alfa made heavy contact near An Dong Lam (YD 680318). After 3 hours of heavy fighting Alfa was ordered to pull back leaving 3 killed in action bodies because of intense fire.

Results:

Friendly: 3 killed in action, 17 wounded in action, 2 missing in action

Enemy: 35 killed in action as battle casualty, 4 wounded in action and taken as prisoner of war, 50 killed in action (estimated)

ARNDT, CRAIG ALAN	SP4	20	08-Mar-68	A CO
BOWERS, WILLIAM JAMES	SP4	20	08-Mar-68	A CO
HUDSON, SAMUEL BERNARD	PFC	19	08-Mar-68	A CO
KIDWELL, WAYNE MINOR	SGT	19	08-Mar-68	A CO
SHRAMKO, MICHAEL ANGELO	PFC	19	08-Mar-68	A CO
STEPHENS, SONNIE	PFC	24	08-Mar-68	A CO
VILLAFRANCO, RODOLFO	SP4	19	08-Mar-68	A CO
WILLIAMS, BENHAROLD	PFC	18	08-Mar-68	A CO

9 Mar - Battalion conducted joint 3 company assault on village complex center of mass YD6731. Alpha, Bravo, and Charlie remained in heavy contact from 09:00 hours to 14:45 hours. Air Strikes, artillery, naval gunfire, and organic weapons, used against suspected 2 battalions of North Vietnamese Army in villages.
Results:
Friendly: 3 killed in action, 17 wounded in action, 2 missing in action.
Enemy: 35 killed in action and taken as battle casualty, 20 killed in action (estimated)

CLEWLOW, ROBERT LEE	SGT	19	09-Mar-68	A CO
HOOD, JOHN EDWARD	SP4	18	09-Mar-68	C CO
VAZQUEZ, WILLIAM	SP4	20	09-Mar-68	C CO
KINNARD, DANIEL LEE	SP4	18	09-Mar-68	HHC

March 10th - Companies engaged in heavy contact in vicinity of YD6731. Charlie and Alfa recovered 5 missing in action, changed to killed in action. Alfa reported finding 38 more bodies from yesterday's action and killed 10 more.
Results:
Enemy: 46 North Vietnamese Army killed in action as battle casualty. 3 wounded in action and taken as prisoner of war.

March 11th - Battalion conducted joint operations and swept Ap Duc Trong with South Vietnamese Regular Army. Contact was light and South Vietnamese Regular Army found 46 North Vietnamese Army killed in action as battle casualty by artillery and captured 3 more.

Results:
Enemy: 46 North Vietnamese Army killed in action as battle casualty by artillery, 3 wounded in action and taken as prisoner of war.

March 12th - Battalion continued operations and made light contact.
Results:
Enemy: 2 Vietcong killed in action as battle casualty, 1 Vietcong taken as prisoner of war.

March 13th- Battalion made light contact during the day and an ambush from Charlie fired on 70 -80 North Vietnamese Army with artillery.
Results:
Enemy: 3 North Vietnamese Army killed in action as battle casualty, 25 wounded in action (estimated)

March 14th - Continued operations and moved companies to landing zone Sally for marshalling and stand down.
MC CONNELL WILLIAM WALKER SP5 26 14-Mar-68 HHC

March 15th - Continued operations and found 1 North Vietnamese Army killed in action as battle casualty by small arms, one day old. Received credit for 48 North Vietnamese Army killed in action as battle casualty by artillery on March 11.
Results:
Enemy: 49 North Vietnamese Army killed in action as battle casualty.
BLEVINS DANNY EUGENE PFC 18 15-Mar-68 B CO

March 16th and 17th - Battalion conducted limited operations and made negative contact.

March 18th - Battalion conducted full operations but made little contact until Delta spotted 10 Vietcong around a fire at 21:30 hours in vicinity (575287). With Popular Forces, the Delta element surrounded and

opened fire on the Vietcong.
Results:
Enemy: 6 killed in action as battle casualty, 3 wounded in action and taken as prisoner of war, 1 killed in action (estimated).

March 19th - Alfa, Bravo, and Delta remained at Sally. Charlie moved to (615235) and began preparing fire support base Strike. No contact.

March 20th - Limited search and destroy operations around Sally conducted. Fortification of fire support base Strike continued.

March 21st - Limited search and destroy operations continued. Alfa ambushed 10 Vietcong and later found a small tunnel complex.
Results:
Enemy: 5 Vietcong killed in action as battle casualties, 2 Vietcong wounded in action and taken as prisoner of war.

March 24th - The Battalion made only light contact except for Delta which received heavy fire from village at (YD618198). All available fire support was utilized.
Results:
Friendly: 1 killed in action, 8 wounded in action, 1 missing in action.
Enemy: 3 killed in action as battle casualty, 10 killed in action, 5 wounded in action and taken as prisoner of war.
JONES BENJAMIN ALLEN SP4 20 22-Mar-68 A CO

This is where my story begins in Vietnam

March 26th – (Not found in the Daily report, the following information is provided from Memory) Captain Greg Mills established a small 4.2 mortar fire support base Lyon. C company was flown in to guard fire support base Lyon and B company was in the valley to the West of fire support base Lyon 629223 (hill 285) in heavy contact with the enemy.

An error in adjustment of the 4.2 mortar fire resulted in heavy casualties. Retired General Cushman, 2d Battalion Commander at the time, recalled this as the worst memory of his military career.

ARMSTRONG EDWIN LAWRENCE	**PFC**	**20**	**26-Mar-68**	**B CO**
BENN PHILIP CRAIG	**2LT**	**22**	**26-Mar-68**	**B CO**
DERRICO JACK EDWARD	**SP4**	**20**	**26-Mar-68**	**B CO**
GIBBLE ALVIN RALPH	**PFC**	**20**	**26-Mar-68**	**B CO**
HORTON JOHN RICHARD	**PFC**	**21**	**26-Mar-68**	**B CO**
HUBBARD GLEN DAVID	**SP4**	**18**	**26-Mar-68**	**B CO**
KREK PHILIP JAMES JR	**SGT**	**21**	**26-Mar-68**	**B CO**
KRUEGER WAYNE DALE	**PFC**	**20**	**26-Mar-68**	**B CO**
LINK ROGER MARK	**PFC**	**21**	**26-Mar-68**	**B CO**
SMITH JOE WILKINS	**PFC**	**19**	**26-Mar-68**	**B CO**
TERRY HOYLE JR	**PFC**	**21**	**26-Mar-68**	**B CO**
BARNES JOHN HOWARD	**SGT**	**22**	**27-Mar-68**	**B CO**

March 28th - Battalion continued search and destroy operations and experienced several changes in command personnel.

    Major Shachnow went to S3 (battalion operations officer)

    Captain Greenhouse went from D to S2 (security)

    Captain Speedy went from C to assistant S3

    1 Lieutenant Wise went to C as Commanding Officer.

    Alfa Company's operational control to 3d Marine Division

March 29th, 30th, 31st - The Battalion continued search and destroy operations in Quang Dien District and defense of An Lo Bridge and landing zone Sally. Very light contact was made with negative results.

WEST JAMES OSCAR	**PFC**	**23**	**31-Mar-68**	**A CO**
YELVERTON DON JUNIOR	**SP4**	**18**	**31-Mar-68**	**B CO**

Results from Dec 19th 1967 to April 1st 1968

Friendly: 48 killed in action, 333 wounded in action, 4 missing in action

Enemy: 613 killed in action as battle casualty, 26 wounded in action and taken as prisoner of war, 210 killed in action (estimated).

April 1st - Company "A" operational control to 3d Marine Division. The other units conducted normal operations with negative results.

April 2nd - Company "A" operational control to 3d Marine Division. Company "B" captured 2 tax collectors in village vicinity YD5731. They also destroyed 3 bunkers and 3 Vietcong killed in action. Company "D" had 1 man injured by boobytrap.

April 3rd - Company "A" returned to the battalion from 3d Marine Division. There was negative enemy contact in the Battalion.

April 4th - A day of light contact with company B receiving sniper fire in vicinity YD5927. Negative friendly or enemy casualties. Company "D" had a grenade thrown in their perimeter. They engaged with small arms resulting in 1 Vietcong killed in action.

April 5th - Company "A" provided mine sweep on QL#1 from An Lo to Camp Evans. 1 platoon moved by truck to vicinity YD6030 to act as a blocking force in support of company B conducting reduction in force from vicinity YD5829 to vicinity YD6127. They engaged only 1 sniper but had 1 US killed in action and 3 wounded in action from boobytrap. They found boobytraps, a sub machine gun, 3 B40 rockets and several other small arms.
RHODES GARY ARTHUR SGT 20 05-Apr-68 B CO

April 6th - A day of light contact throughout the battalion. Company "D" engaged 10 Vietcong in the vicinity of YD4840 resulting in 3 Vietcong killed in action.
CHARETTE MARK OWEN SGT 19 06-Apr-68 B CO

April 7th - Company "D" continued searching area in the vicinity of YD4864 resulting in 5 Vietcong killed in action. The other units conducted search and clear operations and ambushes with negative contact.

April 8th - Company A found an arms cache while conducting reduction in force in the vicinity of YD5325. They found 3 M1 rifles, 1 sub machine gun, 160 rounds for small arms. Company "B" received automatic weapons fire in the vicinity of YD6025, suffering 2 wounded in action. They returned fire with unknown results. Company "C" remained at Camp Evans preparing for future operations and conducting training.

April 9th - Company "A" received their log in vicinity of YD5425. Shortly thereafter they moved approximately 200 meters northeast. Early the next morning 50 Vietcong attacked deserted log sight using long cane poles to flip satchel charges. Company "A" made contact with the enemy suffering 2 killed in action and 1wounded in action. Company B found 9 122mm rockets (complete).
Enemy losses were 2 Vietcong killed in action.
COUGHLIN PATRICK CHARLES   PFC   19   09-Apr-68   A CO

April 10th - Company "A" night defense position in the vicinity of YD5325 received satchel charges, rocket propelled gernade rounds, and small arms fire. Negative casualties. They returned fire with unknown results. Company D conducted security of Phong Dien Bridge and local ambushes. One of these ambushes in vicinity of YD4937, engaged 4 Vietcong with negative results. Recon killed 3 Vietcong in vicinity of YD 5231.

April 12th - The only contact was by company B. They engaged 5 Vietcong in vicinity of YD5830 with negative results.

April 13th – April 13th is the day that 1/502 Infantry was released from the mission of security of Camp Evans. The command post moved from Camp Evans to landing zone Sally.

April 14th - The day was a day of relaxation for the battle-weary troopers of 1-502 as they had stand down at Wunder Beach.

April 15th - A day spent in completing the move to landing zone Sally. The units took re-supply and prepared for future operations.

April 16th - The battalion went operational control to the 1st Brigade until April 30th. During this operation the records were destroyed in a rocket attack.

BELL REGINALD CONRAD	**SP4**	**19**	**16-Apr-68**	**D CO**
HESS ROBERT JAY	**PFC**	**19**	**18-Apr-68**	**D CO**
WILLIAMS REGINALD JR	**PFC**	**23**	**18-Apr-68**	**D CO**
ALFRED THOMAS SAMUEL	**PVT**	**18**	**23-Apr-68**	**C CO**
BROWN DAVID ALLEN	**SP4**	**18**	**26-Apr-68**	**C CO**
INTIHAR JOHN THOMAS	**PFC**	**20**	**28-Apr-68**	**A CO**
KOVALOFF JOSEPH THOMAS	**SGT**	**20**	**29-Apr-68**	**A CO**
LUTZ LARRY EUGENE	**PFC**	**20**	**30-Apr-68**	**A CO**
TERRY ARIE	**CPL**	**24**	**30-Apr-68**	**A CO**

May 1st - Battalion moved back into Quang Dien District by helicopter and began reduction in force operations and security of An Lo Bridge and clearing of Q.L.#1. "C" sprang an ambush at (706348) on 5 North Vietnamese Army, killing 2 as battle casualty. Later 2 Vietcong were captured as they walked into the night perimeter defense. After interrogation it was learned that they were going to vicinity 715330 to act as guides for North Vietnamese Army. At 05:30 hours the night defense position received small arms fire and suffered 1 wounded in action. At 06:35 hours they moved to the village (715330) and swept it finding a grave approximately 24 hours old with 4 killed in action. Results:
Friendly: 1 wounded in action
Enemy: 6 North Vietnamese Army killed in action as battle casualties,

2 wounded in action and taken as prisoners of war.

Alfa returned from operational control to 1-501 Infantry after 3-day operation (Battle of Phuoc Yen). They received credit for 80 North Vietnamese Army killed in action as battle casualties.

DALEY DANIEL WILLIAM	**PFC**	**20**	**01-May-68**	**A CO**
GOMEZ GELASIO NICANOR JR	**SSG**	**29**	**01-May-68**	**A CO**
HOUSE JOHN BURNS	**2LT**	**22**	**01-May-68**	**A CO**
MERSCHEL LAWRENCE JAMES	**PFC**	**20**	**01-May-68**	**A CO**
JACKSON HERMAN	**SGT**	**23**	**03-May-68**	**A CO**

May 4th - Cordon (surrounding an area) by A, B, and Recon with other 2nd battallion elements at vicinity 692303. Contact was heavy during the night by elements seeking to escape the Cordon. Artillery was called for and adjusted as well as use of small arms. At first light a sweep of the area revealed; Enemy: - 26 North Vietnamese Army killed in action as battle casualty, 2 Vietcong killed in action as battle casualty, 3 Vietcong taken as prisoner of war.

May 5th - Battalion continued reduction in force and security missions. A & B cordoned village in vicinity of 700304 and had 1 wounded in action from grenade while enemy losses were 1 North Vietnamese Army killed in action as battle casualty, 2 North Vietnamese Army wounded in action and taken as prisoner of war.

May 6th - Battalion continued its pacification operations. A company night defense position was under sporadic contact from 03:35 hours till 05:45 hours and had 2 wounded in action from small arms fire, from estimated reinforced squad. First light check revealed 1 North Vietnamese Army killed in action as battle casualty.

B company established 3 ambushes. At 21:40 hours one ambush fired on 4 North Vietnamese Army across the river from them. No Assessment could be made. At 07:45 hours another ambush fired on 5 North Vietnamese Army in a sampan (small boat). Results, 5 North Vietnamese Army killed in action as battle casualties and sampan sunk.

Bravo combat assault village in vicinity of 750291 and encountered heavy fire. Formed a cordon of the village with Delta and called in air strikes and artillery.

C company ambush killed 2 North Vietnamese Army killed in action as battle casualty.

Delta combat assault to 748294 and were pinned down by heavy fire. Went into cordon with Bravo suffering 2 killed in action, 7 wounded in action.

Results:

Friendly: 2 killed in action, 9 wounded in action

Enemy: 8 North Vietnamese Army killed in action as battle casualty, 4 North Vietnamese Army killed in action (estimated).

BROGDON DONALD RAY	CPL	18	06-May-68	A CO
MARTINEZ JOHN ANDREW	SP4	20	06-May-68	A CO
THREET HOWARD ANDREW	CPL	20	06-May-68	A CO
HESSION PATRICK B	PFC	18	06-May-68	D CO
QUAN KENNETH RAYMOND	PFC	20	06-May-68	D CO
MC LEMORE TILGHMAN RICHARD	CPT	27	06-May-68	HHC

May 7th - Bravo swept village at first light, vicinity 750290 and made contact. Results, 3 wounded in action, 5 North Vietnamese Army killed in action as battle casualty. Charlie made contact at 08:00 hours and remained in contact throughout the day, vicinity 748307. There was heavy machine gun, light machine gun, automatic weapons and small arms fire. Called in artillery and air strikes.

Results:

Friendly: 2 killed in action, 11 wounded in action, 4 missing in action (later confirmed and recovered as killed in action)

Enemy: 5 North Vietnamese Army killed in action as battle casualty.

CLARK JERRY WAYNE	PFC	22	07-May-68	C CO
DEIKE ROBERT JAMES	PFC	20	07-May-68	C CO
JEFFRIES MACK SIMPSON	SGT	22	07-May-68	C CO
MYERS BILLY EUGENE	SGT	21	07-May-68	C CO
VICTOR GEORGE M	SFC	49	07-May-68	C CO

WILLIAMS DONALD WINSLOW   CPL   24   07-May-68   C CO

May 8th - Battalion continued reduction in force and security missions
of An Lo and QL #1.

"A" made contact at YD715294. Cordoned the village and called in air
strikes.

"B" Company sprung an ambush on 30 North Vietnamese Army with
organic weapons. First light revealed 16 North Vietnamese Army
killed in action as battle casualty.

"C" Company suffered 2 killed in action and 2 wounded in action from
sniper fire.

MORAN JOHN FRANCIS   SGT   22   08-May-68   C CO
FORDI MICHAEL JOSEPH   CPL   20   08-May-68   HHC

May 9th - Bravo found 15 North Vietnamese Army killed in action as
battle casualties from air strike at 724294.

Charlie combat assaulted to YD715302 and made heavy contact,
suffering 2 killed in action and 3 wounded in action. Established
ambushes around the area of contact and captured 1 North Vietnamese
Army who crawled up to one of the positions while trying to escape.

Delta made moderate scattered contact during the day and killed 8
North Vietnamese Army as battle casualties.

Recon found 3 North Vietnamese Army killed in action as battle
casualty in a grave at YD723311.

Results:

Friendly: 2 killed in action, 2 wounded in action.

Enemy: 26 North Vietnamese Army killed in action as battle casualty,
1 prisoner of war taken.

JONES EVERETT SORRELL SSG   28   09-May-68   D CO

May 10th - Battalion continued reduction in force and security
missions in area of operations and made moderate to heavy contact.

Charlie had a running fight with 2 North Vietnamese Army snipers
that led into a village at 7?9333, where they received heavy fire that

killed their point man and prevented his recovery. Air strikes were called in and caused 10 North Vietnamese Army to leave their bunkers and run into Charlie's positions.
Results:
Friendly: 1 killed in action, 1 wounded in action, and 1 missing in action (later changed to killed in action),
Enemy: 1 North Vietnamese Army killed in action as battle casualty. Delta made contact at 715328 and called for an air strike. After the strike a sweep of the area revealed 13 North Vietnamese Army killed in action as battle casualty.
Recon found 8 North Vietnamese Army killed in action as battle casualties at 720296, killed by air strike, the day before.
Results:
Friendly: 1 killed in action, 1 wounded in action, 1 missing in action (Later recovered as killed in action).
Enemy: 32 North Vietnamese Army killed in action as battle casualty.
COOLEY SHELBY EMERSON   PFC   22   10-May-68   C CO
PATTERSON LARRY GENE   SP4   18   10-May-68   C CO

May 11th - Light contact was made during the day and Charlie recovered their missing in action, now killed in action, and found 1 North Vietnamese Army killed in action as battle casualty.

May 12th, 13th and 14th - Light contact made during this time as the Battalion continued the reduction in force and security missions in the area of operation. On the 14th, Recon and Bravo operating with Popular Forces from Quang Dien, killed 1 North Vietnamese Army and 2 Vietcong as battle casualty.

May 15th, 16th and 17th - Light contact made as the battalion was credited with 6 Vietcong killed in action as battle casualty and 2 Vietcong taken as prisoner of war.
LUMAN RONNIE DEAN   SP4   21   17-May-68   C CO

May 18th and 19th - Light contact and the Battalion received 2 wounded in action from snipers.

May 20th and 21st - The Battalion continued the reduction in forces operations and security mission of An Lo and QL#1. During those 2 days only light contact was made.
Results:
Friendly: 1 wounded in action
Enemy: 4 Vietcong killed in action as battle casualty, 1 Vietcong wounded in action (escaped)
Delta, while conducting the road sweep from An Lo to Evans, spotted a mine but before they could remove it a civilian bus ran over it. Results, no one injured but the bus was heavily damaged.

May 22nd - Bravo Company, while on a reduction in force in vicinity 694305, received fire from the village. After returning fire and artillery, they swept the area and found 2 North Vietnamese Army killed in action as battle casualties and captured 5 North Vietnamese Army/Vietcong as prisoners of war in their bunkers.
Delta fired artillery on suspected enemy positions then swept through the area and found 3 Vietcong killed in action and 1 North Vietnamese Army killed in action.
Results: 3 North Vietnamese Army killed in action as battle casualty, 5 prisoners of war taken.

May 23rd, 24th and 25th - Battalion made light contact throughout the period while conducting reduction in force and security missions throughout the area of operation.
Results from these operations were:
Friendly: 1 wounded in action from a booby trap
Enemy: 8 Vietcong killed in action as battle casualty.

May 26th - As the battalion continued operations in the area of operation, Charlie suffered 6 wounded in action from a boobytrap and

105mm round. Delta made heavy contact in vicinity 691312. They returned fire and called in artillery and estimated the enemy element as an North Vietnamese Army company. 14 wounded in action.
Results:
Enemy: 20 wounded in action

May 27th - The Battalion made light contact during the day's operations.
Results:
Friendly: 1 wounded in action from a boobytrap, 1 killed in action from a boobytrap.
Enemy: 1 Vietcong killed in action as battle casualty, 1 Vietcong taken as prisoner of war.
MILLER VERNELL HENRY JR   PFC : 18 : 27-May-68 : C CO

May 28th, 29th, 30th and 31st - The Battalion continued reduction in force operations in the area of operations and security mission of An Lo Bridge and QL#1. During this period contact was very light and resulted in 7 Vietcong captured with weapons.
Results from December 19th 1967 to June 1st 1968:
Friendly: 59 killed in action, 393 wounded in action
Enemy: 852 killed in action as battle casualty, 250 killed in action (estimated), 129 wounded in action and taken as prisoner of war.

June 1st - Light contact. Bravo Company caught 2 Vietcong coming out of bunkers. 2 Vietcong killed in action as battle casualty.
Delta company ambushed 6 Vietcong; 1 Vietcong killed in action.
Later found 2 more trying to run away. 2 Vietcong killed in action.

June 2nd - Battalion reduction in force with Popular Forces. Bravo joint reduction in force with Popular Forces vicinity YD7140. Found that almost all of the gates entering the village were boobytrapped with grenades. These grenades were blown in place. As they swept through the village, they received light contact and returned fire, wounding 1

Vietcong who fled. They also blew several boobytraps in place, but 1 Popular Force was killed when he stepped on a 105mm boobytrap.

June 3rd - Battalion continued operations. Alfa secured An Lo and conducted reduction in force with 1 platoon of Popular Forces, at vicinity YD6231. Popular Forces attacked and killed 3 Vietcong and had 3 wounded in action.
Bravo combined operations. Sweep resulted in 1 wounded in actin from fire at vicinity YD7132 and 3 North Vietnamese Army killed in action in bunkers at vicinity YD7131, by hand grenade.
Recon 1 killed in action by 105mm boobytrap.

June 4th - Battalion continued operation and road sweep. Co B conducted a combat assault to vicinity 699288 and conducted search and cease operations with negative contact.

June 5th - Contact was light, with 2 Hoi Chanh's coming into Co. A's night defense perimeter. They had 1 AK-47 and 1 SKS (semi-automatic rifle manufactured in Soviet Union).

June 6th - Battalion continued operations with Delta working with Rome plow (bulldozer). Contact was light, capturing 1 Vietcong, and 10,000 pounds of rice, 1 SKS and 2 Vietcong killed in action and wounding 1 more who escaped.

June 7th - Battalion continued search of villages in the area of operation.

June 8th - Was a day of heavy activity with all units reporting at least light contact. The Battalion killed 4 Vietcong, captured 4 Vietcong and 2 M-16, 1 AK-47, 1 Czech machine gun and ammo. US troops had three slightly wounded by shrapnel. Two of the Vietcong captured was in a sampan hauling rice down the river. They said that Vietcong used this method quite often.

June 9th - Companies "C" and "A" combined for a cordon search of an area in vicinity YD7030. The cordon resulted in 2 Vietcong killed in action and a large cache containing weapons, ammo, clothing and food. There were 23 bunkers in the area, 15 had been used recently; all destroyed. In vicinity YD7133 numerous punji pits were encountered. Co. C found 5 tons of rice.

Co D and Popular Forces continued operating with Rome plow. Their progress report showed 200 meters of hedgerow, 45 bunkers destroyed. During the day, 8 Vietcong killed in action, 6 Vietcong captured, 1 of these was a messenger who had a document from his commander stating his men could not fight due to lack of food, weapons, and ammo. There were 5 friendly wounded in action from boobytrap.

June 10th – Company's "C" and "A" continued sweep of cordon established June 9th while D Co. continued Rome plow operations. They requested and received an air strike in vicinity YD6931. Company's "C" and "A" had light contact, capturing 7 Vietcong and 5 tons of rice while they had 1 friendly killed in action and 4 wounded in action. The Rome plow destroyed another 36 bunkers. The psychological operations plane flew over the area of operations making leaflet drops and loud speaker broadcasts.

MILLER LARRY T :   PFC : 23 10-Jun-68 : D CO

June 11th - The cordon operation was completed with 6 more Vietcong and 1 Hoi Chanh killed in action, 9 ½ tons of rice were discovered. Also, a directive came out on this day from Brigade that said all elements operating independently would have compass, map, radio, and strobe light.

Co. "A" had one friendly wounded in action (US).

COLLINS TOBY ERNEST : PFC : 20 : 11-Jun-68 : E CO

June 12th - Very light contact. 2 Vietcong killed in action. Company "C" found 19 tons of rice. 1 Popular Force was wounded in action by a boobytrap.

June 13th - The Popular Forces joined Company A and B in a joint operation resulting in 5 Vietcong killed in action, 5 Vietcong captured, 2 AK-47's, 1 M-16, and 1- B40, were captured. 1 Popular Forces and 1 US were wounded in action. Company D continued to support Rome plow which destroyed 5 acres of village, 75 bunkers, and 300 meters of hedgerow.

June 14th - Battalion continued search and clear operations in area of operation and security of An Lo Bridge. Light contact with 1 Vietcong killed in action. 8 Vietcong's and 1 North Vietnam Army captured, 1 Vietcong captain. The Vietcong killed in action was a lieutenant. The Rome plow continued operations, destroying 100 meters of hedgerow and 20 bunkers. Alfa also destroyed 20 bunkers and a small cache.

June 15th - A cordon and a sweep of the village in vicinity YD6432 2 was conducted. The area was heavily boobytrapped. As a result, 1 man was wounded in action, and 2 killed in action.
C Company had 5 killed in action. Akin was a new replacement who just arrived in the noon supply chopper. Everett Carter, who was in Sally when the casualties were reported, rejoined C Company who had been moved to An Lo Bridge to regroup after heavy casualties, believed Akin was killed in action as Akin hadn't had a chance to be known yet. An air strike was requested to destroy boobytraps in the village.
Bravo Company was in contact being under mortar fire and small arms fire most of the day. They killed 5 Vietcong and captured 3 Hoi Chanh's. Rome plow continued destroying 450 meters of hedgerow, 5 acres of village and 70 bunkers.

AKIN JOHN VINCENT   **PFC 20 15-Jun-68 C CO**
DAVID MICHAEL DENNIS   **SP4 24 15-Jun-68 C CO**

FRANCK RALPH HENRY JR   PFC   20   15-Jun-68   C CO
HOYT ARTHUR JAMES   SGT   23   15-Jun-68   C CO
VALENZUELA OSCAR   PFC   20   15-Jun-68   C CO

June 16th – Company "A" initiated ambush, killed 3 Vietcong, captured 2 Vietcong who were wounded in action and 2 AK47's. Company "D" was released from Rome plow and "A" assumed Rome plow security. Rome plow destroyed 500 meters of hedgerow and 88 bunkers. Popular forces conducted patrols and had light contact. 2 friendly wounded in action. Company "B" had 2 wounded in action **BERNARD THOMAS D   PFC   21   16-Jun-68   B CO**

June 17th – Company "C" combined with tanks for reduction in force in vicinity of YD6233, with negative contact. Company "A", with Rome plow destroyed 93 bunkers, 400 meters of hedgerow and uncovered 3 bodies. One Vietcong was detained. Company "A" had 1 US wounded in action.

June 18th - Company "C" and tanks conducted reduction in force. Tanks were utilized to recon by fire and fired canister rounds at suspected booby traps. "A" Company continued Rome plow security. Rome plow destroyed 650 meters of hedgerow and 120 bunkers. "D" Company and Popular Forces conducted joint operation at vicinity YD6930, finding 5 Vietcong bodies and 1 SKS, at vicinityYD6930. Popular Forces with "D" killed 1 Vietcong.

June 19th - Battalion continued operations with very light contact. Killed 1 Vietcong. Rome plow destroyed 80 bunkers.

June 20th - Battalion continued search and clear operations. 6 Vietcong killed in action (one of these was district economic chief) captured 3 AK44's, 1 Czech machine gun, and 1 SKS.
"A" security for Rome plow. Rome plow destroyed 400 meters of

hedgerow and 90 bunkers.

June 21st - Company "C", Company "D", and 1 South Vietnamese Regular Army Company combined for a search and clear operation in vicinity YD7232.
Results:
Enemy: 1 Vietcong killed in action, 3 Vietcong captured, 7 weapons captured.

June 22nd - The 4/3 South Vietnamese Regular Army Battalion operated in our area of operations. While moving into position they were ambushed and later mortared, receiving 6 killed in action and 10 wounded in action. Popular Forces killed 6 Vietcong, captured 1 AK47, 1 AK44, 1 SKS, and 1-90mm. In this operation the Popular Forces platoon leader was killed in action.

June 23rd - Joint operations were conducted with South Vietnam Army and Popular Forces; light contact. Popular Forces captured 7 Vietcong in a sampan boat.
"A" Company captured 1 Vietcong in night defense position. He was Hoi Chanh (North Vietnamese soldier who defected and went to the South under the amnesty program). He then helped "A" and Popular Forces look for the rest of his unit. South Vietnam Army had 2 men wounded in action by booby trap and 1 by small arms fire.

June 24th - Battalion continued search and clear operations. Very light contact. Enemy is becoming very evasive.
Results: 1 Vietcong killed in action,
                5 tons of rice seized.

June 25th - Very light contact. A night perimeter defense was probed on ground and mortared.
2 friendly wounded in action.

3 Vietcong were captured and 2 Hoi Chanh's.

June 26th - A joint operation by A and B Company's was conducted with B blocking vicinity YD7132 and A sweeping, from south towards their blocking position.
Results:
B killed 6 Vietcong and captured 2.
A killed 2, Vietcong and captured 1, along with several weapons.

June 27th - The Battalion conducted defense of An Lo, Rome plow security, and search and clear operations. Very light contact.
US captured 2 Vietcong
Popular Forces received 6 Hoi Chanh. They said all their leaders had been killed by airborne. There were 2 US wounded in action from booby traps.

June 28th - Company B set up blocking position while Popular Forces conducted eagle flight. Resulting in B killing 6 Vietcong.
Popular Forces killed 4 Vietcong, captured 3 Vietcong
Delta Company had 1 killed in action and 6 wounded in action as result of booby traps.
HEISER EDWARD MICHAEL SP4 18 28-Jun-68 D CO

June 29th - Company A conducted reconnaissance in force with Popular Forces.
Captured 1 Vietcong and SKS. Found 2 tons of rice and 1 Vietcong killed in action by artillery.
Company B continued working with Rome plow. Rome plow destroyed 500 meters of hedgerow, 400 meters and 100 meters of village and 83 bunkers.

June 30th - Company A set up blocking position on northwest side of village in vicinity YD6832, while Popular Forces swept through, from southeast, resulting in 3 Vietcong killed in action, 5 Vietcong captured. Company C, had 1 killed in action and 1 wounded in action by booby trap.

July 1st - Battalion continued search and clear operation. Elements from "Pistol Pete" (Sweet Banner 65), Popular Forces, Recon and Alfa combined in a joint operation in vicinity YD6338. Results:
2 Vietcong killed in action
Later 1 North Vietnamese Army and 1 Vietcong Hoi Chanh to "A".
Popular Forces with "A" killed 3 Vietcong, captured 3 Vietcong.
GREGOIRE MILES ROBERT   SGT   18   01-Jul-68   C CO

July 2nd - Battalion continued operation with 5 tanks attached to "D", 4 Rome plows to "B". Contact light with 1 Vietcong killed in action, 1 US and 1 Popular Forces wounded in action by booby trap.

July 3rd - Because of heavy booby traps in vicinity YD6129 artillery preps followed by air strikes were used prior to troops entering the area.
Company "C" got 1 Vietcong killed in action, had one wounded in action from sniper fire.
Company "A" had 3 wounded in action by a Chi Com stick grenade.
"A" captured 3 Vietcong.
WEISTER RONALD KEITH   PFC   21   03-Jul-68   D CO

July 4th - Battalion continued operations with security for An Lo, mine sweep and search and clear operations. One eagle flight was flown (armored helicopter). An air strike was called in on vicinity YD6029. Contact was light. 3 Vietcong killed in action, 3 bodies (2 Vietcong and 1 North Vietnamese Army) killed in action by artillery were discovered buried. The Battalion encountered many booby traps suffering 4 wounded in action and fifteen tons of rice were recovered from cache.

July 5th - Battalion continued search and clear, and Rome plow operation. Resulting in 3 Vietcong killed in action and 4 Vietcong captured. A Hoi Chanh was taken up in a chopper for psychological operations purposes.
1 US killed in action by booby trap and 1 wounded in action.
TEMPLETON GARY DALE   PFC   20   05-Jul-68   A CO

July 6th - Light contact was made. "B" had 1 wounded in action from booby trap and Popular Forces had 1 killed in action from booby trap. Several weapons and small caches were found and 1 Vietcong killed in action.

July 7th - A busy day with Company "A" working to resettle refugees. The Battalion flew eagle flights and one combat assault in vicinity YD6930.
Total results were:
10 Vietcong captured/wounded in action,
4 Vietcong killed in action and 1 North Vietnamese Army captured.
One eagle flight observed cache, with 10 SKS's and 60mm tube.
Numerous other small arms were captured by Battalion.

July 8th - Very light activity in area of operation. Refugees still being moved. 1 Vietcong captured. Popular Forces got 3 Hoi Chanh's.

July 9th - Light sporadic contact throughout the area of operation. Popular Forces combined with US in joint operation including 2 separate combat assault's. The results were 3 Vietcong killed in action, 10 Vietcong captured, 3 Hoi Chanh, and numerous caches and equipment discovered.

July 10th - Although Battalion conducted full scale operation with Popular Forces, making 2 combat assault's, the enemy was elusive. Several weapons were found, 4 North Vietnamese Army killed in action and 1 Vietcong killed in action.

July 11th - Operations continued with Company "D" securing An Lo and working with dozer. "C" searching in vicinity YD6530 for caches. Other units conducted search and clear operations. Light contact with 1 Vietcong killed in action and 2 Hoi Chanh's. The Hoi Chanh said they had given up because of the Rome plows and eagle flights. They said 20 other Vietcong fled to the mountains, that day.

July 12th - Company "D" continued Rome plow operation south of An Lo on the west side of the river. They continued to destroy bunkers, buildings, and found small caches. "A", "B", and "C" continued search and clear operation with light contact. Company "A" had 2 US wounded in action by booby traps. Company "B" found excess of a ton of rice and captured 1 Vietcong in vicinity of YD7132. One Hoi Chanh, turned himself into Company "B".

July 13th - Company "B", Recon and Popular Forces established cordon around village in vicinity of YD6438, with Sweet Banner 65 to sweep from the south.
The totals were:
Company "B": 4 Vietcong killed in action; 4 weapons captured.
Popular Forces: 19 Vietcong killed in action, 16 weapons and 4 Vietcong captured.
Company "D" continued Rome plow work.
Company "C" found 5 tons of rice.
HILL RANDALL STEVEN SP4 19 13-Jul-68 A CO

July 14th - Company "A" continued reconnaissance in force in vicinity YD6026 to YD6128. They had 2 US wounded in action by booby trap. Company "B" and Recon, combat assaulted to YD6929 and YD7029, and continued search and clear operation. Company "C" searched and cleared, vicinity YD6630. Sweet Banner 65, in vicinity YD6334, had contact. Killed 7 Vietcong and captured 2 Vietcong. They also found

12 AK44's, in one cache.

COX FRANK WILLIAM JR		1LT	30	14-Jul-68	A CO
MC CLAFFERTY JAMES EDWARD	SGT	24	14-Jul-68	A CO	

July 15th - The Battalion continued operations in the same locations. The enemy is becoming more evasive and less willing to fight. The day had very little enemy activity. 2 Hoi Chanh's turned themselves into Popular Forces.

July 16th - Company "A" security of An Lo and Rome plow. Company "B", Recon and Popular Forces are still working in the fishhook area center of mass YD7029. They found 9 Vietcong killed in action, 2 North Vietnamese Army killed in action. They also discovered 20 North Vietnamese Army killed in action in plastic bags in the river, in vicinity of YD7029. This is further evidence of the blows dealt to the Viet Cong/North Vietnamese Army.

July 17th - Company "B" continued search and clear in Phouc Yen village. They discovered 6 SKS, 3 AK47's, 1 Chicom 9mm pistol, 1-82mm mortar, various ammo and communication equipment and 7 North Vietnamese Army killed in action. They also killed 2 Vietcong by ambush. Recon conducted combat assault in vicinity of YD6129. Landing Zone was Red and door gunner on gunship wounded in action, enemy broke contact and fled.

July 18th - Company "A" security of An Lo and Rome plow. Company "B" continued search and clear in fishhook area finding several weapons and misc. gear.
Company "C" and 2 platoons of Popular Forces conducted reconnaissance in force in vicinity YD6528. Company "D" reconnaissance in force in vicinity YD6530.
An air strike was called in vicinity YD6332.
Later assessment: 5 Vietcong killed in action.

Popular forces had 3 Hoi Chanh's. Gunships killed 9 Vietcong in vicinity YD6434.

MOORE RONNIE GENE   SP4   20   18-Jul-68   C CO

July 19th - Battalion continued to secure An Lo and conduct search and clear operations with light contact.

Company "C" found 4 tons of rice in vicinity YD6630.

Company "D" had sniper fire (in-effective), enemy broke contact and fled.

Recon received 3 60mm mortar rounds with negative casualties.

July 20th - Company "D" sprung an ambush on 2 Vietcong. Killed 1 Vietcong. Company "A" secured An Lo Bridge. "B","C", and "D" continued search and clear operations with negative contact.

July 21st - Companies "A", "C", and Recon cordon village in vicinity YD6432 and searched, resulting in 2 North Vietnamese Army killed in action and 1 North Vietnamese Army captured. Also captured weapons and destroyed booby traps in the area. CS gas (a riot control gas; burns the eyes) was dropped from a helicopter after the cordon was set up. Company "B", reconnaissance in force in vicinity YD7231, wounded 1 Vietcong. Company "D" sprung ambush on vicinity YD6129 on 1 Vietcong, negative assessment.

July 22nd - Battalion continued search and clear operations. Company "A" made contact with 2 Vietcong in vicinity YD6132 with negative results. Company "B" sprung ambush in vicinity YD7132 resulting in 1 Vietcong killed in action, 2 Vietcong wounded in action, 10 Vietcong captured. "B" killed 1 Vietcong earlier in vicinity of YD7233.

July 23rd - Company "A" secured An Lo and reduction in force in vicinity of bridge. They killed 2 Vietcong in vicinity YD6132. They also captured 1 Vietcong in vicinity YD6132.

Company "B" continued reduction in force operations in vicinity YD7332 and YD7133. Resulting in 3 Vietcong killed in action, 2 Vietcong taken as prisoner of war. They also captured several weapons.

Company "D" was security for Rome plow. The Rome plow hit a 250# bomb, vic. YD6128, destroying the dozer. The driver was not injured.

24th July - Very light contact with Battalion continuing search and clear operations.

Company "A" defense of An Lo Bridge.

Company "B" detained 11 Vietcong's in vicinity YD7233 (later classified as I Corps).

Company "C" had 1 US wounded in action and 1 Vietcong killed in action in vicinity YD6323.

July 25th - Company "A" secured An Lo Bridge and assisted in security of Rome Plow.

Company "C" with 1 platoon of Popular Forces, found 1 Vietcong killed in action by artillery.

Company "B" and "D" continued search and clear operations with negative contact.

July 26th - Battalion continued search and clear operations with all companies receiving at least sniper fire. When fire was returned, the enemy fled. The Vietcong are now in smaller groups. 1 US, from "C" Company was wounded by boobytrap.

July 27th - Company "A" secured An Lo Bridge and mine sweep. Company "B" conducted joint operations with 7 platoons of Popular Forces. Reduction in force to village C/M, YD6830 with blocking positions at YD6729 and YD 6333. Then 4 platoons of Popular Forces combat assaulted in vicinity YD6629.

Totals for the day:

Safe in the Perimeter of His Hands

Popular Forces: 1 Vietcong killed in action, 7 Vietcong captured and numerous weapons.

"B" Company: 9 Vietcong killed in action. One of these was C114 Company Commander, and later a female Vietcong (Quang Dien LNO) was killed.

Company "C", reduction in force in vicinity YD6132 and YD6333. They hit 250# booby trap. Results: 4 wounded in action (scout dog killed in action) at vicinity YD6232. They captured 4 Vietcong's.

July 28th - Company "A" secured An Lo Bridge. Company "B" conducted reduction in force to village C/M YD6828, where a few small caches were found and numerous boobytraps but negative contact. Company "C" no caps. Company "D", operational control moved to 1st Batallion. Popular Forces combat assaulted to YD7029. Reduction in force to village C/M YD7030. Results: 3 Vietcong killed in action (1 was platoon leader and another assistant platoon leader of Tan Taun Lai.)

July 29th - Company "A", secured An Lo Bridge and mine sweep. Company "B" conducted reduction in force operations to village C/M vicinity YD6829. Results, 11 Vietcong killed in action (gunships killed 3 more in vicinity YD6530), 3 Vietcong taken as prisoner of war and 1 Chieu Hoi.

Company "C", Rome plow security.

Company "D", operational control moved to 1st Battalion. Popular Forces combat assaulted vicinity YD6631 and YD6530 and conducted sweep and block for Company "B". Results, 2 Vietcong killed in action, 4 Vietcong and 1 AK47, captured.

July 30th - Battalion continued search and clear operations with negative contact. Battalion concentrated on caches and boobytraps. A total of 6 Chieu Hoi's surrendered.

July 31st - "A" Company secured An Lo Bridge. "B" continued

reduction in force. "C" had contact in vicinity YD6431 but enemy fled. Company "D", operational control moved to 1st Battalion. Recon received 2 rocket propelled grenade rounds in vicinity of YD6432 but never saw enemy.

August 1st - Company "A", secured An Lo Bridge and established local ambushes.
Company "B", reduction in force in vicinity YD6529.
Company "C", Rome Plows security.
Company "D", sprung ambush in vicinity YD6930, on 2 Vietcong, 1 Vietcong killed in action. Log bird fired on 3 North Vietnamese Army in vicinity YD2331.
Recon moved into the area finding 1 North Vietnamese Army killed in action and 2 North Vietnamese Army wounded in action.

August 2nd - Battalion continued normal operations with Company "A" securing An LO Bridge, mine sweep, and local patrols. One ambush killed 1 Vietcong in vicinity YD6339. Patrols killed 2 Vietcong in vicinity YD6833 and captured 2 Vietcong in vicinity YD6334.
Company "B" conducted combat assault to vicinity YD6928 and captured 2 Vietcong in vicinity YD6334.
Company "B" conducted combat assault to vicinity YD6928, with negative contact.
Company "C", Rome Plow security.
Company "D", operational control moved to 1st Battalion.

August 3rd - Battalion conducted normal operations with company "B" killing 1 Vietcong in spider hole.

August 4th - Company "A" secured An Lo Bridge, reduction in force to village in vicinity YD6432. They encountered boobytraps but no Vietcong.
Company "B", reduction in force C/M, in vicinity YD6630. They killed 1 Vietcong and captured 3 Vietcong, in vicinity YD6432.

Company "C" received small arms fire from village in vicinity YD6232 and called artillery, with negative assessment.
Company "D", operational control, 1 327. Recon reduction in force in vicinity YD6836.

August 5th - Company "A" secured An Lo Bridge and conducted eagle flights to the north, into "Street" area. Company "B" killed 3 Vietcong and captured 2 while on reduction in force operation in vicinity YD6630.

August 6th - Battalion continued reduction in force operations and secured An Lo Bridge. Several small caches were discovered, and Company "C" killed 1 Vietcong.

August 7th - Battalion conducted reduction in force operations. Company "C" conducted combat assault and engaged 1 Vietcong with negative assessment.

August 8th - Battalion continued with reduction in force operations. Company "C" conducted combat assault and Recon had established ambushes. Recon had light contact with 3 Vietcong, negative assessment.

August 9th - Intensive operations, including eagle flights by Company "B" and combat assault by Recon.
Total for the day were: 2 Vietcong captured by Company "B". "B" also come under mortar attack and had 3 wounded in action.

Aug 10th - Company "A" secured An Lo Bridge and established ambushes. They sprang ambush, in vicinity YD6131, resulting in 2 North Vietnamese Army captured. The North Vietnamese Army said they were from the 9th North Vietnamese Army regiment. "A" Co. encountered many boobytraps resulting in 2 killed in action and 2 wounded in action.

"B" Company reduction in force in vicinity YD6534. Company "B" killed 1 Vietcong and captured 2 while conducting reduction in force operation to vic. YD6334. They continued RIF to the south, finding a base camp. Resulting in 5 VC KIA, 5 VC captured and 3 VC. Several weapons were also captured. Later while in NDP, "B" Co. was mortared, hit with SA fire and RPG. "B" Co. had 1 KIA and 11 WIA.

OLENZUK PAUL GREGORY   **PFC 22 10-Aug-68 A CO**
VALKER GEORGE ERNEST 3RD   **SP4 21 10-Aug-68 A CO**
KRISKOVICH RAYMOND GEORGE   **SP4 24 10-Aug-68 B CO**
HAYNES ALBERT RANDELL   **PFC 20 10-Aug-68 E CO**
SNYDER MICHAEL BRYANT   **SP4 21 10-Aug-68 E CO**

August 11th -16th - Battalion continued reduction in force, security of An Lo Bridge, and Rome plow operations with very light contact. Company "A" was taken off of An Lo security and "B" Company replaced them. Company "D" is at fire support base Georgia.

FINK PHILIP RUSH 1SG 41 13-Aug-68 A CO

August 17th - Company "A" received 60mm mortar fire, in vicinity YD6133. They called for artillery, but first light check proved negative assessment. Company "B" secured An LO Bridge and worked with Rome plow.

August 18th - Contact was light with "B" Co. capturing 2 Vietcong. 1 Vietcong wounded in action and was brought into command post by his parents. He was evacuated to 22d Surgical.

August 19th - Company "C" detained 3 Vietcong while conducting reduction in force operation, in vicinity YD6334. While moving Vietcong to a landing zone, one Vietcong detonated a boobytrap, injuring all 3 Vietcong and 2 US. Company "D" received several mortar rounds at fire support base Georgia, resulting in 1 US wounded in action.

August 20th - Company "A" conducted reduction in force in vicinity, YD6131 with negative contact. Company "B" secured An Lo and security of Rome plow. Company "C" discovered 3 Vietcong bodies, in vicinity YD6333 that had been result of Company "A's" action on July 27th.
Company "C" also captured 1 Vietcong wounded in action in vicinity YD6433.
LAWHORNE DONNIE JACKSON   SP4   19   20-Aug-68   B CO

August 21st-22nd - Contact extremely light. Company "D" was sent to landing zone Sally for rapid reaction force duty. They utilized this time to get new equipment and resupply.

August 23rd - Company "A" reduction in force in vicinity YD6133. They were utilizing local sampans to search river and one capsized. 1 US drowned. Company "B" security of An Lo and Rome plow operation. Company "C" conducted combat assault to vicinity YD6031.
Results were 3 Vietcong killed in action, 1 Vietcong and 2 Cheiu Hoi's captured.
Company "D", killed 2 Vietcong in vicinity of YD6729 in bunkers.
GOODEN JOHNNIE   SGT   19   23-Aug-68   D CO

August 24th - Company "A" engaged small Vietcong force in vicinity YD6133 with small arms. Negative assessment. They also engaged 6 sampans resulting in 2 Vietcong killed in action.
Company "B" secured An Lo. The enemy tried a small-scale ground attack which was repelled. Negative casualties.
Company "C" conducted reduction in force in vicinity YD6333, killing 2 Vietcong in vicinity YD6729 in bunkers.

August 25th - Received a report that C114 LF Vietcong company was located in a village in vicinity YD6830. Company "D" was sent to cordon the area. Early that morning 7 Vietcong tried to swim the river.

Results: 7 Vietcong killed in action. 1 other Vietcong killed in action in river later. A search of the village the next day resulted in no enemy being found.

August 26th - Company "A" reduction in force operation and Rome plow security. They found 2 Vietcong in bunker. They had been dead about a week. No other contact.

August 27th - Company "A" sprang ambush on 2 Vietcong in vicinity YD6123, resulting in 1 Vietcong killed in action. Received 3 rocket propelled grenade rounds in vicinity YD6131, 3 US wounded in action. There was light contact with 2 other groups of Vietcong (2-3). 1 Vietcong killed in action in vicinity YD6134.
Company "B" continued security of An Lo. They captured 1 Vietcong female in vicinity YD6334.
Company's "C" and "D" continued reduction in force operation with negative contact.

August 28th - Battalion continued normal operation. The only contact was by ambushes. Company "C" called artillery on approximately 9 Vietcong, 400-500 meters northeast of vicinity YD6033, with negative results.
Company "D" observed movement in front of their ambush. They fired small arms and threw grenades, resulting in 1 Vietcong killed in action.
HOOK MARK LOREN   PFC   18   28-Aug-68   C CO

August 29th - Very light contact. 1 Vietcong was captured in a bunker by Company "A", working with Rome plow.

August 30th - Company "A" conducted reduction in force in vicinity YD5132, resulting in 1 Vietcong killed in action and 16 Viet Cong's captured. Recon made contact in vicinity YD6830. They engaged 2 Viet Cong, but they fled. Company "B" killed 2 Viet Cong, wounded 2

Viet Cong, while operating in vicinity YD6438.

August 31st - Company "A" was the only unit to have contact. They killed 1 Viet Cong in vicinity YD6830.

September 1st - An ambush by company "D" engaged 1 VC, vic. YD6730, resulting in 1 VC KIA and a weapon. Recon was sent to vic. YD7231, where log bird had fired on 3 NVA. Recon got 1 North Vietnamese Army killed in action, 1 North Vietnamese Army and 1 Viet Cong captured.

September 2nd - No significant contact but the Battalion continued to encounter many booby-traps.

September 3rd - Company "A" found 2 Viet Cong bodies in a bunker in vicinity YD6232. Company "B" found about 3000 pounds of rice. Recon found 2 Viet Cong graves.

September 4th-5th - No contact was made. Company "C" replaced company "A" on An Lo Bridge security.

September 7th - Company "A", killed 1 Viet Cong and captured 2 in vicinity YD7030. Company "B" found weapons cache with 26 weapons in vicinity YD6234. Company "C" secured An Lo Bridge and established local ambushes. Recon killed 2 Viet Cong and captured 1 Viet Cong in vicinity YD7334.

September 8th - Company "A" captured 2 female Viet Cong in vicinity YD7030. They killed 2 Viet Cong and captured 2 in vicinity YD6556 The Viet Cong fled, dropping 2 weapons. Blood trails were found but no bodies.
Company "B" killed 1 Viet Cong and discovered 18 individual weapons and 8 machine guns in vicinity YD6234.
Recon killed 2 Viet Cong in vicinity YD7333.

WHELAN MICHAEL PATRICK SGT 20 08-Sep-68 E CO

September 9th - Very light contact. Company "B" sprang an ambush on 2 Viet Cong in vicinity YD6035, resulting in 2 Viet Cong killed in action.

September 10th - Company "A" continued reduction in force in vicinity YD6630, finding 5 tons of rice, killing 1 Viet Cong in a bunker and capturing 2 Viet Cong's. "A" Co. engaged 5 Viet Cong in vicinity YD6730 from ambush. Negative results.
Company "C" moved to fire support base Mongoose, operational control to 1/501.
Company "D" moved to An Lo Bridge to assume bridge security.

September 11th - Company "A" conducted reduction in force in vicinity YD6631.
Company "B" sprang an ambush in vicinity YD6133 on 2 Viet Cong, resulting in 1 Viet Cong killed in action. This Viet Cong was tax a collector. "B" Company also had security of Rome plow and reduction in force operations with negative contact.
Company "C" operational control to 1/501.
Company "A" secured An Lo, local patrols around bridge. They detained 1 Viet Cong.
Recon ambushed 3 Viet Cong, killing 1 in vicinity YD7031.

September 12th - Company "A" engaged 2 Viet Cong in a bunker in vicinity YD6729. 1 killed and 1 captured. They had contact with 2 or 3 Viet Cong, twice more but negative assessment.
Company "B" continued Rome plow security and reduction in force operations with negative contact.
Company "C", operational control 1/501.
Company "D" security of An Lo.

September 13th - Company "A" continued reduction in force operation

297

in vicinity YD6731, capturing 1 Viet Cong. While on Rome plow security, "B" Company received small arms fire in vicinity YD6332. A cordon was formed around the village and artillery was called in. A sweep of the area resulted in 9 Viet Cong killed in action and 10 Viet Cong taken as prisoner of war, and several weapons. One of the prisoner of war's was the Commanding Officer of the H319th and another cadre finance officer was captured.

September 14th - Company "B" continued cordon, calling in artillery and air strikes. Final results for the day were 8 Viet Cong killed in action, 11 Viet Cong taken as prisoner of war. The other units continued normal activity with negative contact.

September 15th-17th - Battalion continued reduction in force operations, Rome plow operation, and security of An LO Bridge. The enemy was evasive and there were only two light sniper contacts, with negative assessment. The units continued to encounter booby traps and find small caches.

September 18th - Company "A" sprung an ambush in vicinity YD6729 on 1 Viet Cong, resulting in 1 Viet Cong killed in action. Company "B" provided security for Rome plow. Company "C" still operational control to 1/501.

September 19th - Company "D" had light contact with 2 Viet Cong in vicinity YD6630 with negative results. Recon engaged 5 Viet Cong in vicinity YD7130 with negative results. They later engaged 1 Viet Cong from ambush in the same area, resulting in 1 Viet Cong killed in action.

September 20th - Company "A" security of An LO. Company "B", operational control to 1/501. Company "C" reduction in force in vicinity YD6530. They had 2 light contacts with 3 Viet Cong in vicinity YD6628 and 4 Viet Cong in vicinity YD7029, with negative assessment.

September 21st-23rd - Normal activities continued with no contact. Company "B" found 1 ammo cache in vicinity YD6029.

September 24th - Battalion continued reduction in force operation. Company "B", operational control to 1/501. Company "D" killed 2 Viet Cong in vicinity YD6234. Recon engaged 2 Viet Cong in vicinity YD6913 resulting in 1 Viet Cong captured.

September 25th - Company "A" security of An Lo and local patrols and ambushes. Company "B" on operation at Phu Vang. Company "C" and "D" continued reduction in force operation. Recon captured 1 Viet Cong in vicinity YD6930

September 26th - A day of very light contact. The only unit to make contact was company "D". They ambushed 2 Viet Cong, resulting in 2 Viet Cong killed in action.

September 27th-28th - The Battalion continued normal combat operations, but there was no enemy contact, in these two days.

September 29th - Company "A", security of An Lo and mine sweep. Company "B" had movement near one of their ambushes in vicinity YD6532. They engaged with small arms fire, with negative results. A look-out on the tower at An Lo, spotted 15 individuals, digging-in. Artillery was called in, results unknown.

September 30th - Company "C" replaced company "A" on An Lo Bridge security. Company "C" conducted reduction in force operation in vicinity YD6731. Company "B" detained 7 Viet Cong's in vicinity YD6135.

Safe in the Perimeter of His Hands

October 1st - Company "A" conducted reduction in force in vicinity YD6530. They engaged 2 Viet Cong with small arms fire, resulting in 1 Viet Cong killed in action. One of their day ambushes killed in action 1 Viet Cong in vicinity YD6928. Company "B" engaged 3 Viet Cong with small arms fire and clamors in vicinity YD6031, with negative assessment.

October 2nd-3rd - No enemy activity or contact during this period.

October 4th - Company "A" set up blocking positions in vicinity YD6729 for 2 platoons sweeping from southeast. Company "B" had 2 Cheiu Hoi's lead them to an arms cache, containing 2 60mm mortars and 18 individual weapons, 1000 rounds of ammo, 8 clamors (Chi Com), 10 rifle grenades, and 2 rocket propelled grenade rounds. Company "C" received 2 mortar rounds at An Lo. Negative casualties. Recon had stand-down at landing zone Sally.

October 5th - Company "A" conducted reduction in force and ambushes in vicinity YD6730 with negative contact. Company "B" found 1 SKS, ammo and other equipment in vicinity YD6538. At vicinity YD6130, Company "B" engaged 1 Viet Cong with negative assessment. Company "D" at Phu Vang.

October 6th - The Battalion (with the exception of "D", at Phu Vang) continued normal operations with negative contact. We did provide 4 enlisted men to night perimeter on a check point to look for Viet Cong and draft dodgers. The enlisted men worked with elements from Pistol Pete, from vicinity YD7529 to vicinity YD8332. They detained 183 people who were classified as follows:
IC   131
VCS   9
South Vietnamese Regular Army deserters   1
Military age males   41

Safe in the Perimeter of His Hands

Viet Cong 1

October 10th - Negative contact.

October 11th - Company "A" is at Phu Vang. They have security for one/S on highway 551 and occupied strong points along POL pipeline, security of pumping station, Hue Bridge and LCU ramp.
Company "B" reduction in force in vicinity YD6929 and night ambushes.
Company "C" security of An Lo and local patrols and ambushes.
Company "D", reduction in force in vicinity YD6629. Killing 1 North Vietnamese Army in a bunker and captured 1 Viet Cong.
Recon had negative contact.

October 12th - Company "A" still at Phu Vang, with the same mission. Company "B" and "C" continued reduction in force operation and ambushes with negative contact. Company "D" captured 4 Viet Cong in vicinity YD6629 in bunkers. They also captured 2 M-16, 1-.45 pistol and a light machine gun. Recon continued reduction in force and night ambushes with negative contact.

October 13th - Company "A" operating at Phu Vang. Company "B" had one wounded in action in vicinity YD6930 by sniper. They returned fire but had negative assessment. Company "C" security of An Lo, mine sweep and local patrols and ambushes. Company "D" receiver small arms fire in vicinity YD6628. They returned fire with small arms, machine gun and M-79. A sweep of the area produced 4 Viet Cong killed in action. Recon captured documents from a sampan in vicinity YD7233. The Viet Cong's in sampan escaped.

October 14th - The Battalion continued reduction in force and ambushes with negative contact. The documents found on one of Company "D's" killed in actions's, of October 13th, showed that one of them was a company commanding officer, Hoang Van Trung, of

K300B.

October 15th - Company "B" was only unit to have contact. They engaged 2 Viet Congs in sampans in vicinity YD7129, resulting in 2 Viet Cong killed in action.

October 16th - The Battalion had negative enemy contact on this day. It was, however, an important day as it was the day we assumed security of fire support base T-Bone. Company "C" lifted to T-Bone at 16:00hrs.

October 17th-18th - TIR missions, ambushes and eagle flights, failed to develop contact.
MASON JAMES PHILLIP   SP5   19   17-Oct-68   HHC

October 19th - Battalion continued reduction in force operation, security of An Lo, T-Bone and company "A" at Phu Vang. No contact made. Company "C" found small cache in vicinity YD7230

October 20th - Company "A", at Phu Vang. Company "B" security of An Lo and mine sweep. The 1/3 South Vietnamese Regular Army regiment, working in our area of operation in vicinity YD6529, found 2 Viet Cong bodies attributed to company "D", 8 days ago. Company "D", engaged 3 Viet Cong in vicinity YD6438, with small arms fire. Negative assessment. Company "C", 36 elements, at T-Bone.

October 21st- Negative enemy contact. Psychological operations personnel, led by Chu Hoi, captured 60mm mortar. Two PACV's from Pistol Pete, started operating in northeast part of our area of operation, bounded by Song Bo and Jung Rivers. They picked up 1 Viet Cong. Our S-3 acted as aerial observers for this operation.

October 22nd - Company "A", at PhuVang. Company "B" security of An Lo and mine sweep. Company "C" worked with PACV's from

---

Pistol Pete. Company "D" was the only unit to make contact. They engaged 3 Viet Cong wounding 1. The other 2 fled carrying the wounded with them.

October 23rd - Company "B" while on An Lo Bridge security, engaged 1 Viet Cong with small arms. Negative assessment. The S-3 air sighted 2 Viet Cong from log bird and engaged, resulting in 2 Viet Cong killed in action and 2 weapons.

October 24th - Company "A" lifted from Phu Vang to vicinity YD8130. Company "B" security of An Lo. Company "C" lifted from T-Bone to Phu Vang to assume security mission of company "A".

October 25th - The only unit making contact was company "D". They engaged 2 Viet Cong with negative assessment. They found 3 cases of rocket propelled grenade rounds and other ammo in vicinity YD6453.

October 26th - Company "A" detained 1 Viet Cong in vicinity YD7132. Company "B" security of An Lo Bridge. Company "C" Phu Vang. Company "D" operational control to 1/501, "C" Company, 26 element, T-Bone. Recon fire support base Apache.

October 27th - The Battalion had negative enemy contact. The last light recon flight engaged 1 Viet Cong, unknown results, but captured 10 grenades, 1-.45 pistol, 4 rucksacks and some documents.

October 28th - Company "A" ambushes in vicinity YD7233, received small arms fire. They engaged 2 Viet Cong with negative results. 1 IS wounded in action. Company "B" security of An Lo. Company "C" at Phu Vang. Company "D" operational control to 1/501. "C" Company, 26 element, fire support base T-Bone, security.

October 29th-30th - No contact made.

Safe in the Perimeter of His Hands

November 1st - Company "A" conducted reduction in force operation in vicinity YD6630. Company "B" security of An Lo, mine sweep and local patrols and ambushes. Company "C" Phu Vang, providing security for mine sweep of highway 551, occupied strong points on POL pipeline, security of pump station and LCU ramp. Company "D", operation control to 1/501. Recon at Apache. Company "C", 26 elements, at T-Bone. Negative contact.

November 2nd - The units continued operations in the same vicinity except that Company "D" returned to An Lo and Company "B" went operational control to 1/502. There was negative contact.

November 3rd - Battalion continued normal operations with negative contact.

November 4th - Company "A" reduction in force in vicinity YD6630. Company "B" operational control to 1/501. Company "C" at Phu Vang. Company "D" security of An Lo Bridge. Recon security of fire support base T-Bone. There was negative contact.

November 5th - Company "A" was lifted by "hook" to fire support base T-Bone. Their mission, to provide security and conduct local patrols and ambushes. Company "B" operational control to 1/501. Company "C", Phu Vang. Company "D" security of An Lo, mine sweep and local patrols and ambushes. No contact.

November 6th-7th - Battalion continued normal operations with negative contact. Company "B" returned to landing zone Sally. Company "C" returned from Phu Vang and lifted to vicinity YD5815 for reduction in force operations.

November 8th - This day marks another important day in the history of the Battalion. On November 8th an area of operation extension into the sands area referred to as "the street". Company "B" and 4 platoons of

Safe in the Perimeter of His Hands

Popular Forces conducted a combat assault in vicinity YD5840 and YD6040 and set up cordon with 1 platoon of tanks from which saturation patrols could be run. Naval river patrol boats were used as a blocking force in vicinity YD6041 and YD5942. The command-and-control helicopter drew small arms fire and returned fire on suspected enemy locations with negative results. Company "B" hit a 105 booby trap, injuring 2. Patrol boats detained 5 Viet Cong's but they were later classified as IC and released.

November 9th - Company "A" continued security of fire support base T-Bone. Company "B" continued cordon with Popular Forces and tanks. They received small arms fire in vicinity YD6039 with negative casualties. They returned fire with negative results. They had 1 killed in action and 1 wounded in action from a 105mm booby trap. Company "C" conducted reduction in force operation in vicinity YD5717. Company "D" security of AN Lo Bridge.
LEATUTUFU FAGALII LAITA   SSG   22   09-Nov-68   B CO

November 10th - Company "B" was the only unit to have contact, engaging 2 Viet Cong with small arms fire in vicinity YD6140, resulting in 2 Viet Cong Prisoners of War. They tripped 60mm booby trap, resulting in 3 wounded in action. The 1/502, received a new "First Strike". Lieutenant Colonel Davis replaced Lieutenant Colonel Carter as the Battalion Commander. General Zais, General Trung, several other generals and numerous Division VIP's attended the ceremony at landing zone Sally.

November 11th - Company "A" security of T-Bone, local patrols, and ambushes in the area. Company "B" continued operation in "street" area. They had light contact with estimated 2 Viet Cong but there were negative casualties. Company "C" reduction in force from vicinity YD5818, southeast to vicinity YD5717. Company "D" security of An Lo Bridge. Recon reduction in force from landing zone Sally to

YD6124.

November 12th - Company "A" switched security missions with Company "D". Company "A" lifted, via "hook" from An Lo to fire support base T-Bone. Company "D" lifted, via "hook", from T-Bone, to An Lo. Company "B" engaged 2 Viet Cong from ambush with clamor and small arms fire, with negative assessment. Company "C", form ambushes, observed movement, threw hand grenades, with negative results.

November 13th - Company "A" security of An Lo Bridge. Company "B" had 1 platoon of Popular Forces lifted in via log bird to YD5939. The tanks attached to Company "B", continued to work with unit on reduction in force missions. Company "B" found 1 booby trap (homemade), in vicinity YD6139, resulting in 4 Viet Cong killed in action and 1 Viet Cong prisoner of war. Later, in vicinity YD6238, 2 Viet Cong killed in action in bunker. Company "D" operating in mountains, near fire support base T-Bone, spotted 4 Viet Cong. They called in aerial rocket artillery and artillery with negative assessment. Recon sighted a "red-filtered-light", in vicinity YD6121 and called in artillery with negative assessment.

November 14th - Company "A", while on security mission at An Lo, received 6 rounds of 60mm mortar fire. Negative causalities. Company "B" continued operation in "Street" area, in vicinity YD614?, resulting in 3 Viet Cong killed in action and 4 Viet Cong captured, along with 1 AK47. The Viet Cong were all hiding in bunkers. Company "D" found a cave, in vicinity YD6219 with 1000ft. of detonation cord, 1 mine and ammo.

November 15th - The Battalion continued normal operations with negative contact. All units are conducting classes in spare time as the Battalion is experiencing a large turnover of personnel, returning to continental United States.

November 16th - Company "A" security of An Lo Bridge. Company "B" conducted combat assault from vicinity YD6337 to YD6023. Negative contact. Company "C" lifted, via "hook", from fire support base T-Bone to landing zone Sally for stand-down and resupply. Company "D" lifted, via "hook" to fire support base T-Bone and assumed security of fire support base T-Bone. Recon engaged 3 Viet Cong in sampan, resulting in 2 Viet Cong killed in action and captured 1 AK and 1 .32 cal. Pistol. Recon lifted, via log bird to Omaha.

November 17th - Recon departed Omaha to vicinity YD6038, to establish blocking position. They were joined by 1 tank platoon and 1 Popular Forces platoon. Company "C" combat assaulted to vicinity YD6040 and started sweeping towards the blocking force. At vicinity YD6038, Recon killed 1 Viet Cong.

November 18th - Battalion continued normal operations with negative contact. One of the tanks, operational control to Company "C", hit an anti-personnel mine with negative damage. Company "C" released Recon and tank platoon from operational control and was lifted via "hook" to fire support base Birmingham. They became operational control to 2/501.

November 19th - Company "A" security of An Lo Bridge. Company "B" conducted reduction in force operation in vicinity YD6321 with negative contact. Company "C" operational control to 2/501. Company "D" security of fire support base T-Bone. 1 platoon to 1 Popular Forces company, conducted joint saturation patrols in vicinity YD6724. Recon destroyed 2 bouncing betty mines and captured 4 Viet Cong in vicinity YD6140.

November 20th - Company "A" security of An LO Bridge, mine sweep and local patrols and ambushes. They found 1 bouncing betty mine in

307

vicinity YD6123 and destroyed in place. Company "B" found two 250-pound bombs while conducting reduction in force operation in vicinity YD6231. They destroyed it in place. Company "C" operational control to 2/501. Company "D" security of fire support base T-Bone. 1 platoon of Popular Forces was lifted by log bird to work jointly with Recon in vicinity YD6040.

November 21st- Company "A" sent their 26 elements to fire support base Panther, operational control to 2/501. Company "B" conducted reduction in force to fire support base T-Bone and assumed security mission of T-Bone. Company "C", operational control to 2/501. Company "D" conducted reduction in force to vicinity YD6418. Recon killed 6 Viet Cong and captured 4 Viet Cong, 1 French machine gun, 2 AK47's, and 1 M-79, documents and ammo in vicinity YD6630.

November 22nd - Company "A" lifted from An Lo via "hook" to vicinity YD7133. Recon and "D" Company, 36 elements, security of An Lo Bridge. Company "B" received 2 platoons of Popular Forces to assist in reduction in force operation in vicinity YD6125.

November 23rd - Company "D" found Battalion sized base camp in vicinity YD6318, with 60 bunkers, 20% of which had overhead cover. The area looked like a platoon sized element had used the bunkers in the last 24 hours. Recon and Popular Forces captured 2 Viet Cong in vicinity YD6630. One of them identified 12 Viet Cong supply personnel. They are being checked now.

November 24th and 25th - Company "D" was the only unit to have contact. They engaged 3 Viet Cong in vicinity YD6218, resulting in 3 Viet Cong killed in action.

November 26th - Company "A", lifted via "hook" to fire support base T-Bone and conducted reduction in force to vicinity YD6219. Company "B" security of T-Bone with local patrols and ambushes.

Company "C" released from operational control 2/501 and lifted from fire support base Birmingham to landing zone Sally. Company "D" had contact at YD6120 with 1 Viet Cong. Negative assessment. "D" Company later moved via "hook" to An Lo Bridge and assumed mission of securing bridge.

November 27th - Company "D" engaged 1 Viet Cong in vicinity YD6218 while on reduction in force operation. Results: 1 Viet Cong killed in action. Later in the day, they found 5 graves (results of earlier contact in area) Recon and Popular Forces killed 4 Viet Cong and captured 1 Viet Cong and 5 weapons in vicinity YD6536. Company "C" operational control to 2/501.

November 28th - Company "A", security of An Lo Bridge. Company "B" security of T-Bone, with B16 operational control to 2/501. Company "C" operational control to 2/501. Company "D" killed 2 North Vietnamese Army, captured 1 AK47 and 3 magazines and found 5 graves in vicinity YD6218. Recon conducted reduction in force from vicinity YD6433 to An Lo.

November 29th - The only contact was Company "D". 1 man killed in action by sniper. Company "D" searched the area thoroughly, but the enemy had fled.
PARTSAFAS TERRYL GLENN   SP4   20   29-Nov-68   D CO

November 30th - Company "D" was the only unit to make contact. They engaged 3 Viet Cong in vicinity YD5640. The enemy fled leaving their rifles and equipment. They sighted 5 more Viet Cong but all were out of small arms range.

December 1st - Company "A" conducted reduction in force to vicinity YD6220. They engaged 3 North Vietnamese Army resulting in 2 North Vietnamese Army killed in action and 1 North Vietnamese Army captured, along with 2 AKs, and 1 French machine gun. "A"

Company operational control to 2/501. Company "B" security of T-Bone with "B" Company, 26 element, operational control to 2/501. Company "C" moved by vehicle from landing zone Sally to secure An Lo Bridge. "First Strike", while flying over area of operation saw a Viet Cong. The Viet Cong turned out to be wounded and "First Strike" captured and evacuated via log to 326 medical. (This prisoner of war furnished intelligence very useful in future mountain operations)

December 2nd - Company "A" engaged 2 Viet Cong in vicinity YD6220, resulting in 2 Viet Cong killed in action, 2 AKs, 2 rucksacks and equipment and documents captured. Company "B" security of T-Bone with local patrols and ambushes. "A" Company, 26 element and "B" Company, 16 element, operational control to 2/501. Company "C" security of An Lo. Company "D", Company "C" 16 element, Recon, 1 tank platoon and 2 Popular Forces platoons (operational control to "D") established a cordon, center of mass in vicinity YD595390. Several boobytraps were encountered, resulting in "C" Company 16 platoon leader killed in action and 2 Popular Forces wounded in action. 2 Viet Cong were killed in action. 1 Viet Cong captured with 2 AK47. The cordon also found 1 60mm mortar, 1 rocket propelled grenade, a machine gun and approximately 700 pounds of rice.
WEISSMAN VICTOR BARRY 1LT 21 02-Dec-68 C CO

December 3rd - Company "A" conducted reduction in force in vicinity YD6220. They received sniper fire from the northwest. The fire was returned with negative assessment. "A" Company, 26 element, operational control to 2/501. Company "B" security of T-Bone. Company "C" security of An Lo Bridge. Company "D", with Recon, platoon of tanks and Popular Forces continued cordon operations. They found 1 fresh Viet Cong grave (killed in action by artillery) and 1 bouncing betty mine. Popular Forces killed 2 Viet Cong and captured 1 weapon in vicinity YD6338.

December 4th- The only significant activities were by Company "D" as the cordon continued. They found 2 rocket propelled grenade rounds and 2 anti-personnel mines. Shortly after noon the cordon was terminated. Recon conducted move via "hook" from vicinity YD5034 to Omaha. From Omaha, they conducted combat assault to vicinity YD6928.

December 5th - The Battalion continued normal operations. The only unit to make contact was Company "D". They engaged 2 Viet Cong in vicinity YD5934, resulting in 1 Viet Cong killed in action and 1 AK47 captured. Recon was lifted back to landing zone Sally from vicinity YD6829, by log bird.

December 6th - Company "A" moved from vicinity YD6120 to fire support base T-Bone. "A" Company 36 element was lifted via "hook" from landing zone Sally to T-Bone. Company "A" replaced Company "B" as T-Bone security. Company "B" reduction in force from T-Bone to vicinity YD6519. While moving into their night defense position. Company "B" observed movement in vicinity YD6417 and called in artillery. A first light assessment proved negative. Company "C" security of An Lo Bridge. "C" Company 16 element with 1 platoon of Popular Forces conducted reduction in force to vicinity YD6132 where they set up a blocking position for 2 platoons of Popular Forces. They conducted a combat assault to vicinity YD6134, then swept towards blocking positions. There was negative contact. Company "D" conducted reduction in force operations in vicinity YD64537. Recon at landing zone Sally as ready reaction force for Battalion.

December 7th - Company "A" secured fire support base T-Bone and conducted local patrols and ambushes. Company "B" conducted day and night ambushes in vicinity YD6518. Company "C" secured An Lo Bridge, security for mine sweep, and conducted local patrols and ambushes. Company "D" conducted reduction in force to vicinity YD6040. They engaged 2 Viet Cong resulting in 1 Viet Cong wounded in action and 1 M-26 and rucksack captured. Recon remained at landing zone Sally.

December 8th - Although Recon was the only unit to make contact (they engaged 1 Viet Cong at their night defense position with negative results), the Battalion conducted several unit moves by "hook". Company "C" moved from An Lo to vicinity YD6922. Company "D" moved from vicinity YD6139 to An Lo. Recon moved to vicinity YD6139 from landing zone Sally.

December 9th - The only unit to have contact was the Recon platoon. They sprung an ambush on 1 Viet Cong at vicinity YD6139, resulting in 1 Viet Cong killed in action. Another ambush at vicinity YD5939, killed 2 Viet Cong with small arms.

December 10th - On this day we lost the "Street" section of our area of operation to the 3/5 Cav., for an 8-day operation. Recon and "C" Company 26 element, went operational control to 3/5 Cav. for 4 days (10th-13th). The only contact made was by Company "D", when they engaged 3 Viet Cong in vicinity YD6124, with negative results.

December 11th and 12th - Company "A" secured T-Bone. Company "B" conducted reduction in force operations in vicinity YD6118. They engaged 5 Viet Cong while operating in this area, but the Viet Cong fled with negative assessment. Company "C" is operational control to 1/501. "C" Company 26 element, is operational control to 3/5 Cav. Company "D" secured An Lo Bridge. Recon is operational control to 3/5 Cav.

December 13th - Company "A" secured T-Bone with platoon reduction in force in vicinity YD6222. This reduction in force utilized 2 scout dog teams. A "hook" was utilized to move one 4.2 and one 81mm mortar and crew to Apache for practice firing and was then lifted via "hook" to T-Bone. Company "B" reduction in force operations, day

312

and night ambushes in vicinity YD6218. Company "C" is operational control to 1/501. Company "D" secured An Lo Bridge. Recon is operational control to 3/5 Cav.

ROWE SALVATORE ALFRED   PFC   18   13-Dec-68   B CO

December 14th - Company "A" secured T-Bone with 1 platoon on local reduction in force operations. The unit concentrated on rebuilding and improving fortifications of T-Bone and unit training. Unit training is being stressed in all units as the turbulence of personnel has been a point of concern for the Battalion Commander. Company "B" conducted reduction in force in vicinity YD6188. They found a bunker complex (negative signs of recent use) in vicinity YD6117 and destroyed it. Company "C" released from 3/5 Cav. And returned via "hook" to landing zone Sally. Company "D" secured An Lo Bridge. Recon released from operational control to 3/5 Cav. And returned to landing zone Sally, via "hook" to be ready reaction force.

December 15th- Company "A" secured fire support base T-Bone and conducted local patrols and ambushes. "C" Company 26 element was operational control to Company "A". They conducted reduction in force operation from landing zone Sally to vicinity YD6020. While concluding reduction in force they heard a small arms shot. On investigation, they found freshly cooked rice alongside the trail in vicinity YD6121 and later 3 Viet Cong. The Viet Cong fired on Company "B" (negative casualties). Fire was returned and the Viet Cong fled. Gunships were called in on suspected locations. Upon searching the area, negative bodies were found, but they did find 3 hooches which contained various gear, ammo, propaganda material and personal effects. Two blood trails were also found. Company "B", followed the blood trails with negative results. Company "C" is operational control to 1/501. Company "D" secured An Lo Bridge. "D" Company 16 element, combat assaulted to vicinity YD6019 and became operational control to Company "B". Recon moved by vehicle from landing zone Sally to An Lo where they utilized a super contact team.

December 16th - Company "B" had light contact in vicinity YD6119. They engaged 3 Viet Cong resulting in 1 Viet Cong killed in action and 2 Viet Cong wounded in action. "B" Company had 1 US slightly wounded. Company "C" returned to landing zone Sally (from operational control to 1/501) via "hook" from fire support base Sandy. Recon platoon (with 2 platoons of Popular Forces) departed An Lo to reduction in force in vicinityYD6131. "C" Company 26 element, conducted Eagle flight from landing zone Sally to vicinity YD6238. Gunship escort engaged 2 Viet Cong with negative results.
LUDWIG JAMES MICHAEL   PFC   20   16-Dec-68   B CO

December 17th - Company "A" security T-Bone with "A" Company 16 element reduction in force to landing zone Sally. Company "A" was lifted via "hook" from T-Bone to landing zone Sally. Company "B" continued reduction in force operations in vicinity YD6121. "B" Company sprang an ambush in vicinity YD6120 against unknown size enemy element. Illumination and artillery were called in with negative results. Company "C" was lifted from landing zone Sally to fire support base T-Bone. "C" Company 26 element and 2 Popular Force platoons conducted search and clear operation in vicinity YD6139. The area had just been swept by 3-5 task force, but "C" Company 26 element and Popular Forces killed 3 Viet Cong and captured 2 weapons. Company "D" secured An Lo Bridge.

December 18th - On this day there was no enemy contact. Company "B" was lifted via "hook" from vicinity YD6221 to An Lo Bridge and replaces Company "D" on Bridge security. Company "D" moved via "hook" from An Lo to vicinity YD6321.

December 19th - Another day of light contact. One of Company "D's" ambushes received small arms fire. They called in artillery with negative results. "B" Company 16 element, Company "A" and Recon established cordon around villages to the southeast of An Lo, along the Song Bo river. Center of mass in vicinity YD6429. The road QL#1 was blocked off by military police and all traffic checked. The Vietnamese National Police and local Popular Forces swept through cordon.

The results were:

Detained 180

Classified 156 - IC

14 - Draft age men

4 - Deserters

6 - VC

December 20th - Cordon operations were continued the next day with the following results:

Detained 43

Classified 31 - IC

10 - Draft age men

1 - Deserter

1 - Civil Offender

There was negative enemy contact on this day.

December 21st - Company "A" had no actual contact but found one North Vietnamese Army/Viet Cong base camp. The bunkers contained 3 rifles, various cooking utensils, food and ammo. They also found 2 fresh graves (Viet Cong killed in action by artillery) Recon and 2 Popular Forces platoons conducted search and clear operations in vicinity YD6028. They killed 7 Viet Cong and captured 3 Viet Cong. The Viet Cong were all hiding in spider holes and bunkers. Also captured were 3 weapons, ammo, and some documents.

December 22nd- The Battalion continued to conduct extensive reduction in force throughout the area of operation. Company "D" however was the only unit to make contact. They engaged 2 Viet Cong in vicinity YD6119, resulting in 1 Viet Cong killed in action and 1 US wounded in action. "D" Company captured 1 AK47, ammo, and gear. Later in the same area they discovered a cache with small arms ammo, rocket propelled grenade round, 25 pounds of salt and 2 SKS bayonets.

December 23rd - The only contact was by "D" Company as they killed 1 Viet Cong with small arms fire in vicinity YD5921.

December 24th - Very little activity as the Battalion returned to static positions in observance of the Christmas truce, to start at 1800 hours. Early in the morning Company "D" killed 1 Viet Cong from ambush with a claymore.

December 25th - Christmas day found Company "A" at landing zone Sally, Company "B" at An Lo, Company "C" at T-Bone, and Company "D" at landing zone Sally, with Recon at An Lo. The Battalion observed the Christmas truce and enjoyed a Holiday meal.

December 26th - Company "A" conducted a combat assault to vicinity YD6040 and conducted search and clear operations in vicinity of the landing zone. The results were, 1 Viet Cong killed in action, 1 Viet Cong prisoner of war, 3 weapons, 750 pounds of rice, uniforms, gear, ammo, and some documents were captured. The other units resumed offensive combat operations but had negative contact.

December 27th - Company "A" had 7 people wounded in action by booby traps they encountered. Many booby traps in the area of vicinity YD6140. Company "C" operating in vicinity YD6218, found 4 bodies, killed about 3 or 4 days earlier. They also found 2 M-72 LAW's and 1 rocker propelled grenade round. They engaged 2 Viet Cong with small arms in vicinity YD6219 with negative results.

December 28th - Company "A" continued reduction in force operation in vicinity YD6140, finding 300 pounds of spoiled rice and 1 ton of polished rice. Company "D" had 1 US wounded in action by booby trap in vicinity YD6128. They detained two Viet Cong in vicinity YD6326.

December 29th - Company "A" had 2 wounded in action from anti-personnel mines in vicinity YD6334. Company "B" and 2 Popular Forces platoons conducted combat assault to vicinity YD5940. They found and destroyed a booby trap in vicinity YD5940. In the same area they found a bunker, with ammo, magazines, Vietnamese water purification tablets. Later they found a graveyard in vicinity YD5939 with signs stating in Vietnamese, "Stay out Booby Trapped Area".

December 30th - Company "A" secured An Lo. Company "B" conducted reduction in force operation in vicinity YD6040. They destroyed a 105mm round and an 8-inch round and found small (200 pound) cache of rice. At vicinity YD5841 they engaged 1 Viet Cong resulting in 1 US wounded in action. Negative enemy assessment. Company "D" secured T-Bone with 1 platoon ("D"-26) conducting reduction in force around T-Bone. Recon remained at landing zone Sally as ready reaction force.

December 31st - The Battalion continued combat operations but had negative contact. Company "B" found 2000 pounds of rice, 2 Viet Cong in graves (result of Recon's previous contact) and 5 anti-personnel mines.

1969

The 1st Battalion, 502d Infantry was operating in the vicinity of FSB T-Bone and An Lo at the beginning of the year. The mission of the battalion was to provide bridge and mine sweep security at An Lo and conduct reconnaissance in force and search and clear operations in the area of operations. This was part of Operation NEVADA EAGLE, which was being conducted by the 2d Brigade.

On January 25th the battalion began Operation SHERMAN PEAK, which was in support of Operation NEVADA EAGLE. The battalion's mission was to conduct reconnaissance in force operations in the vicinity of fire support base Veghel to locate and destroy enemy forces and installations, prevent enemy infiltration along highways 547 and 547A, and provide protection for engineer reconnaissance teams along highways 547 and 547A. This mission was conducted in conjunction with the 3d ARVN Regiment. This was primarily a spoiling operation to prevent an enemy buildup in preparation for an attack on Hue.

During the period of the operation no significant contact was made nor were there signs of recent enemy activity. However, many caches were found, some of which were believed to be remaining from the Tet offensive of 1968. The caches consisted primarily of ammunition and explosives. Operation SHERMAN PEAK ended on February 9th and the battalion continued to participate in Operation NEVADA EAGLE with the 2d Brigade.

During Operation NEVADA EAGLE the 1-502d Inf conducted training and joint operation with the Popular Forces in Quang Dien District. This proved to be quite successful and as forces proficiency increased the 1-502d Infantry was able to occupy a larger area of operations. Operation NEVADA EAGLE ended on Feb 28th, 1969.

January 1st - The 1/502d Infantry started out the year as a participant in Operation NEVADA EAGLE. Company A provided bridge and mine security at An Lo. Company B conducted operations in vicinity YD585398. C Company conducted operations in vicinity YD610177, YD615192 and YD619190. At YD615192 D Company, 3d platoon, found one 30 caliber carbine and 16 bunkers. D Company provided security at fire support base T-Bone and Recon Platoon conducted operations in vicinity YD641316, YD640326 and YD640320.

January 2nd - A Company provided bridge and mine sweep security at An Lo. A Company, 1st and 2d platoons, conducted reduction in force operations in vicinity An Lo. 2d platoon lifted to landing zone Sally assumed duties as Brigade ready reaction force. B Company conducted search and clear operations in vicinity YD599394. At YD582400 B Company 2d platoon found approximately 1 ton of rice and destroyed it. B Company, 3d platoon found 1 bandoleer of M-16 ammunition and 1 bandoleer of M-79 ammunition at YD56383. B Company, 1st platoon found a homemade booby trap at YD585394. At YD603384 1st platoon found approximately 100 pounds of rice and gave it to the Popular Forces. B Company, 2d platoon found a small cache of medicine at YD595384. C Company conducted reduction in force operations in vicinity YD618190. At YD611192, C Company, 3d platoon found 5 bunkers showing signs of recent use. They also found a fresh latrine, 1 AK magazine, and some food. D Company established night defense positions at fire support base T-Bone. D Company 1st platoon conducted reduction in force operations in the vicinity. Recon platoon conducted reduction in force operations from vicinity YD6829 to vicinity YD7131. The Battalion Surgeon conducted medical civil assistance program at YD736297; 45 Vietnamese attended.

January 3rd - A Company conducted bridge and mine sweep security at An Lo. B Company conducted search and clear operations in vicinity YD597383 with 2 platoons of Popular Force. At YD600377, B Company, 1st platoon, and Popular Forces spotted 5 Viet Cong and called in artillery. A check at first light produced negative results. At YD595383, B Company, 2d platoon found approximately 300 pounds of spoiled rice and destroyed it. B Company, 3d platoon found an antipersonnel mine at YD617389 and destroyed it. C Company conducted a reduction in force operation and day and night ambushes in vicinity YD618201. At 0933 hours at YD605187, C Company, 2d platoon engaged 4 Viet Cong. Viet Cong moved to the west with unknown enemy casualties. At 1045 hours, at the same location, C Company, 2d platoon engaged 1 Viet Cong resulting in 1 Viet Cong wounded in action. Platoon followed blood trails to the south. At 1158 hours at YD611197, C Company, 3d platoon engaged 1 Viet Cong, resulting in 1 Viet Cong wounded in action and 1 AK47 captured, and found a rucksack with documents. At 1250 hours at YD611137 D Company, 2d platoon engaged an 8-man North Vietnamese Army patrol, wearing new uniforms, rucksacks and carrying AK47's. The patrol moved out to the northeast. There were unknown enemy casualties and negative US casualties. At 1437 hours at YD612187, C Company, 2d platoon reported 1 wounded Viet Cong Chieu Hoi. D Company provided security for fire support base T-Bone. 1st and 2d platoons conducted reduction in force operations in vicinity of fire support base T-Bone. Recon platoon conducted reduction in force operations in vicinity YD733333.

January 4th - A Company provided bridge and mine sweep security at An Lo. B Company conducted search and clear operations and day and night ambushes in vicinity YD597383 with 2 platoons of Popular Forces. At YD602388 B Company, 1st platoon found 1 Chicom booby trap and destroyed it in place. At YD584395 B Company, 3d platoon found 20 sandbags full of rice and footprints leading to the north. C Company conducted reduction in force operations in vicinity YD618186. At YD 604195 C Company, 2d platoon found 3 hooches, 1 M79 grenade launcher, 4 chicom grenades, ammunition, North Vietnamese Army clothing, fresh food, and medicine. At 1535 hours at the same location, 2d platoon engaged 1 Viet Cong, resulting in the capture of 1 Viet Cong wounded in action, 1 AK47 and documents. D Company provided security for fire support base T-Bone and 3d platoon conducted reduction in force operations. Recon platoon conducted reduction in force operations in vicinity YD732338. **WESSEL STEVEN ARTHUR PFC 20 04-Jan-69 D CO**

January 5th - A Company located at An Lo provided bridge and mine sweep security. 1st platoon acted as Battalion ready reaction force. B Company conducted search and clear operations with 2 platoons of Popular Forces in vicinity YD5939. C Company conducted reduction in force operations in vicinity YD6118. D Company provided security for fire support base T-Bone. Recon platoon conducted reduction in force operations in vicinity YD6736.

January 6th - A Company continued to provide bridge and mine sweep security at An Lo. 1st platoon conducted reduction in force operations to the south of An Lo. B Company conducted reduction in force operations in vicinity YD6736. C Company conducted reduction in force operations from vicinityYD6120 to landing zone Sally. D Company continued to provide security for fire support base T-Bone. Recon platoon conducted search and clear operation in vicinity YD6537.

January 7th - A Company provided bridge and mine sweep security at An Lo. The company also conducted reduction in force operations and saturation patrols in the vicinity. The company moved to landing zone Sally. B Company conducted reduction in force operations from vicinity YD6736 to Omaha. They made a truck move from Omaha to landing zone Sally. C Company moved by trucks from landing zone Sally to An Lo. 1st platoon conducted reduction in force operations in vicinity YD6432. D Company provided security for fire support base T-Bone. Recon platoon conducted search and clear operations.

January 8th - B Company departed landing zone Sally and conducted reduction in force operations to fire support base T-Bone where they assumed the security of fire support base T-Bone. C Company provided bridge and mine-sweep security at An Lo. D Company departed T-Bone and conducted reduction in force operations. D Company 2d platoon found 1 bouncing betty mine at YD671228 and destroyed it in place. 1 man from Recon platoon was wounded by an unknown type of booby trap at YD613386.

January 9th - The battalion conducted reduction in force operations, with B Company providing security at An Lo and Recon platoon at

321

landing zone Sally for a standdown.

January 10th - The battalion continued with reduction in force operations. B Company provided security at An Lo.

OFFERDAHL WILLIAM BRUCE SP4 19 10-Jan-69 A CO

January 11th - A Company conducted a combat assault from landing zone 653245 to landing zone 588155. At 1955 hours at YD646226 A Company, 2d platoon received automatic weapons fire from 2 Viet Cong. 2d platoon returned the fire. The engagement resulted in unknown enemy casualties and 1 US killed in action, 2 US wounded in action. D Company conducted a combat assault from primary zone YD635245 to fire support base Strike. Recon platoon and mortars were lifted by CH47 from landing zone Sally to fire support base Strike.

January 12th - A Company conducted saturation patrols in vicinity YD5814. B Company provided security for fire support base T-Bone. C Company provided bridge and mine sweep security at An Lo. Recon platoon provided security for fire support base Strike.

January 13th - A Company conducted saturation patrols in vicinity YD5914. At YD600140 A Company, 1st platoon found 8 old foxholes and an old trail. B Company conducted reduction in force operations in vicinity of fire support base T-Bone. C Company continued with its mission at An Lo. At 1000 hours at YD607256, C Company, 2d platoon reported 9 male and 13 female detainees, who were sent to landing zone Sally, classified as IC and released.

January 14th - A Company conducted saturation patrols in vicinity YD5815. At YD585 2d platoon found a campfire 4 to 5 hours old. They checked the area with negative results. B Company provided security for fire support base T-Bone and conducted reduction in force operations in the area. C Company continued with its mission of bridge and mine sweep security at An Lo. At fire support base Strike.

Recon platoon sighted through field glasses 11 Viet Cong at vicinity YD573175. The Viet Cong were engaged with 81mm mortars with negative results.

January 15th - The battalion continued its mission of providing security for An Lo, fire support base T-Bone and fire support base Strike. Reduction in force operations were also conducted.

January 16th - A Company conducted saturation patrols in vicinity YD6015. B Company provided security at fire support base T-Bone with 3d platoon conducting reduction in force operations in the vicinity. C Company provided bridge and mine sweep security at An Lo. D Company conducted saturation patrols in vicinity YD5516. D Company 1st platoon found 1 dud 750-pound bomb at YD561158. It was later destroyed in place by an explosive ordinance disposal team.

January 17th - A Company moved to fire support base Strike and then lifted to fire support base T-Bone. A Company began providing security for fire support base T-Bone. AT YD586174 A Company found an old hooch containing 1 SKS, 1 AK47, 1 M1 carbine and some ammunition. B Company was lifted from fire support base T-Bone to fire support base Strike. D Company moved to fire support base Strike and was then lifted to landing zone Sally. Recon platoon departed fire support base Strike and conducted reduction in force operations.

January 18th - A Company provided security for fire support base T-Bone. 1st platoon conducted reduction in force operations from fire support base T-Bone to vicinity YD6529. B Company conducted saturation patrols in vicinity YD5817. C Company provided security for bridge and mine sweep team at An Lo. 1st platoon conducted reduction in force operations to landing zone Sally. C Company was moved by trucks from An Lo to landing zone Sally. D Company conducted a maintenance standdown at landing zone Sally. They conducted a combat assault from landing zone Sally to landing zone

YD688318, landing zone YD688304, and landing zone YD673305. After completion of the combat assault, D Company conducted search and clear operations in vicinity YD6831, YD6830, and YD6730. E Company established fire support for fire support base Strike. Company was lifted from fire support base Strike to landing zone Sally and fire support base T-Bone. Recon platoon conducted saturation patrols in vicinity YD5816 and YD5817. Psychological operations were conducted in the central area of Quang Dien District.

January 19th - A Company provided security for fire support base T-Bone. They also sent out a platoon sized ambush and platoon sized operations. B Company conducted saturation patrols in vicinity YD5816. At YD588153 B Company, 1st platoon found fresh Ho Chi Minh sandal tracks leading to the north. The tracks were followed with negative results. C Company operational control to 2/501 was lifted from landing zone Sally to fire support base Birmingham. D Company conducted saturation patrols in vicinity YD6830. At YD705310 D Company, 1st platoon picked up 2 detainees, evacuated to Quang Dien district headquarters, classified as IC and released. At YD718319 2d platoon found 1 M26 hand grenade booby trapped. It was destroyed in place. Recon platoon conducted saturation patrols under operational control Company B.

January 20th - A Company continued to provide security for fire support base T-Bone. 3d platoon conducted operations in vicinity YD6421. B Company conducted saturation patrols in vicinity YD5917. At YD592182 B Company 3d platoon found fresh footprints, 2 sampans and a well-used trail running from north to south. At YD588184 3d platoon found a dirt stairway cut into a hillside. At YD588183 3d platoon found three 2-man bunkers and destroyed them. D Company conducted saturation patrols vicinity YD7131. 3d platoon was located at landing zone Sally as Battalion rapid reaction force. Recon platoon under operational control B Company conducted

saturation patrols. At YD580182 Recon platoon found a sampan
landing area and a tunnel, neither of which showed signs of recent use.

January 21st - A Company provided security for fires support base T-
Bone. At 1700 hours, while on a reduction in force operation, 1st
platoon detonated 1 60mm mortar round boobytrap at YD652223. It
resulted in 1 US wounded in action. B Company, with Recon platoon
operational control, conducted reduction in force operations. At
YD594186, Recon platoon received a satchel charge and 9mm pistol
fire resulting in 1 US killed in action. At YD592189 2d platoon found
4 old platoon size hooches which had been recently used and 1
Chicom grenade. At YD593186 2d platoon found 1 reinforced bunker
and some ammunition. At YD596187 Recon platoon found and
destroyed 2 security bunkers and sixteen 55 gal drums of kerosine C
Company remained operational control to 2/501. D Company
conducted saturation patrols in vicinity YD7131. 3d platoon detained 6
male Vietnamese at YD728330. Detainees were sent from district
headquarters to Hue as draft dodgers, and the other four were
forwarded to the national police for interrogation.
WHITE MICHAEL JAMES SP4 19 21-Jan-69 E CO

January 22nd - A Company continued to provide security for fire
support base T-Bone. A Company, 1st platoon conducted saturation
patrols in vicinity YD640220. B Company conducted saturation
patrols in vicinity YD5919. At YD593199 2d platoon found a hole and
small bunker and destroyed them. D Company conducted saturation
patrols in vicinity YD7132. 2d platoon was located at landing zone
Sally as Battalion rapid reaction force.

January 23rd - A Company continued to provide security for fire
support base T-Bone and conducted reduction in force operations in
the area. B Company conducted saturation patrols in vicinity YD5919.
C Company moved via CH47 from fire support base Birmingham to
fire support base T-Bone, was released from operational control 2/501.

D Company conducted saturation patrols in vicinity YD7123 and YD7229. Recon platoon was lifted to landing zone Sally and released from operational control B Company.

January 24th - A Company lifted from fire support base T-Bone to landing zone Sally. 1st platoon conducted reduction in force operation to landing zone Sally. B Company lifted from PZ YD596202 to landing zone Sally. C Company provided security for fire support base T-Bone. D Company was marshalled at landing zone Sally along with Recon platoon.

January 25th - The battalion began operation SHERMAN PEAK in support of Operation NEVADA EAGLE. A Company remained at landing zone Sally as Battalion rapid reaction force. B Company conducted a combat assault from landing zone Sally to fire support base Veghel. Upon approaching fire support base Veghel they received small arms fire. At 1445 hours B Company captured 1 Viet Cong in a bunker at fire support base Veghel. The prisoner of war was evacuated to fire support base Geronimo for interrogation. C Company moved by CH47 from fire support base T-Bone to landing zone Sally. D Company moved from landing zone Sally to fire support base Veghel and then departed fire support base Veghel to conduct reduction in force operations in vicinity YD545030. Departing fire support base Veghel D Company received friendly fire from fire support base Veghel at 1538 hours, resulting in 1 US wounded in action. Battalion tactical operation center command post moved by truck from Omaha to landing zone Sally and then moved by CH47 to fire support base Veghel. D1-501, operational control to 1-502d, conducted a combat assault from fire support base Birmingham to fire support base Bastogne.

January 26th - A Company conducted a combat assault from landing zone Sally to fire support base Zon. The company found various amounts of US ammunition on fire support base Zon and destroyed it.

Safe in the Perimeter of His Hands

B Company provided security on fire support base Veghel. A man was spotted outside the perimeter and engaged with negative results. C Company was lifted from landing zone Sally to fire support base Veghel by CH47. They then conducted reduction in force operations to vicinity YD555126. D Company conducted reduction in force operations from YD545030 to vicinity YD533038. Vicinity YD534026 D Company found three 4-man bunkers, 1 60mm mortar round, and 200 AK47 rounds. At YD531035 they found approximately 5000 12.8mm rounds. At YD533038 D Company found a tunnel complex containing 3 cases of TNT, 800 rounds 12.7 ammunition and wheels for a 50-caliber gun carriage. Recon platoon was operational control to A Company. At YD465003 Recon found 5 small security bunkers and destroyed them. In vicinity YD470998 Recon platoon found 10 bunkers, and 6 spider holes with hooches over the holes. They appeared to be 2-4 weeks old. D Company 1-501 continued to provide security for fire support base Bastogne and conducted local patrols around Bastogne.

January 27th - A Company conducted a reduction in force operation from YD465003 to YD455992. At vicinity YD465003 A Company, 1st platoon found 1 8mm French Bolt action carbine. Vicinity YD470998 A Company found 43 bunkers, 3 kitchens (2 of which were underground) 1 latrine, 1 pick and 1 shovel. 5 bunkers were newly constructed with 4 old fire ashes in the kitchen. B Company continued to provide security for fire support base Veghel. C Company conducted reduction in force operations. At YD559028 C Company found fresh tracks of 3 persons. A search of the area produced negative results. D Company conducted reduction in force operations from YD533038 to YD527037. At YD533038 the company found 1000 AK47 rounds, 350-pound TNT, blasting caps, 100 Mauser rounds, and a M60 machine gun in bad shape. At YD531038 they found 123 boxes of 12.7mm rounds. D-1-501 was located at fire support base Bastogne. The company minus conducted a reduction in force operation with an engineer party to YD800059 and returned to Bastogne.

January 28th - A Company conducted a reduction in force from YD470990 to YD456991. B Company provided security at fire support base Veghel. 2d platoon conducted a reduction in force with engineers along RF 547 and returned to fire support base Veghel. At YD561045 B Company, 2d platoon found 9 85mm rounds, 200 12.7 mm rounds and 100 pounds TNT. At YD559044 2d platoon found 6 old bunkers, 7 destroyed enemy trucks (3/4-ton size) and the remains of a downed helicopter. C Company conducted a reduction in force operation from YD555037 to YD530046. At YD550035 the company found footprints and followed them with negative results. D Company conducted reduction in force operations from YD527037 to YD517045. At YD517045, the company found 4 hooches, 1 kitchen, 1 classroom with signs that read "Training Center" and "Attack Enemy", 3 small bunkers, 1 latrine and 1 lookout tower. D-1-501 provided security at fire support base Bastogne. At 2230 the company received automatic weapons fire from southwest of Bastogne from an estimated enemy force of 10. They also received 4 rocket propelled grenade rounds. D Company returned fire with small arms and artillery. There were no friendly casualties.

January 29th - A Company conducted reduction in force operations in vicinity YD4599. B Company conducted reduction in force operations in the vicinity of fire support base Veghel. In vicinity YD529036 2d platoon found an old bunker complex with commo wire running throughout it. At YD554046 1st platoon found an abandoned ammunition cache containing 240 7.62mm rounds, one 75mm HE round, 500 rounds of 25mm AA- ammunition, 12 60mm mortar fuses, three 75mm fuses, 400 empty Russian rocket boxes, 300 60mm cases, 300 82mm cases, 50 82mm fuse cans, 15 aiming posts, twenty-five 55 gallon fuel drums. Also, they found 50 heavy bunkers, 150 fighting bunkers, tracks from wheeled and tracked vehicles, a strip of corduroy road, and 10 ammo dumps. Companies C and D conducted reduction in force operations. D-1/501 continued to provide security for fire support base Bastogne.

January 30th - A Company conducted a reduction in force from YD457995 to YD460002. At YD460000 3d platoon found 9 old bunkers, at YD458002 they found 17 old bunkers and at YD458997 found 6 old bunkers. At vicinity YD458997 1st platoon found 2 small bunkers and vicinity YD450002 3d platoon found 2 bunkers with 101 pounds TNT and 200 electric blasting caps. B Company provided security for fire support base Veghel and conducted reduction in force operations in the vicinity. At YD554047 1st platoon found 2-75mm rounds in box and metal cannister. Vicinity YD531041 3d platoon found 3 bunkers containing 10 sealed cases of 12.7mm ammunition. C Company conducted reduction in force operations. Vicinity YD536061 the company found three 60mm rounds. At YD542067 the company found old bunkers and two 82mm rounds. D Company conducted reduction in force operations in the vicinity of YD5006. Recon platoon was operational control A Company. At YD462008 Recon found 18 small foxholes, 1 bunker, 1 pick and 2 North Vietnamese Army shovels. D-1-501 continued to provide security for fire support base Bastogne and conducted squad size patrols around Bastogne.

January 31st - A Company continued with reduction in force operations. At YD456016 2d platoon found bombed out AA gun position containing 4 12.7mm rounds. B Company provided security at fire support base Veghel. 2d platoon and 3d platoon conducted reduction in force operations in vicinity YD545048 2d platoon found 600 rounds M60 ammunition, two 60mm rounds and 1 CS gas grenade. Companies C and D conducted reduction in force operations with negative results. Recon platoon was operational control A Company. Recon found three 55 gal drums of gasoline with Russian lettering. D-1-501 continued to provide security for fire support base Bastogne and conducted a mine sweep to fire support base Birmingham.

February 1st - A Co conducted a saturation patrol. In vicinity YD483025 2d platoon found 1 complete truck engine, 2 engine blocks and 1 footlocker of uniforms without insignia (buttons had Chinese writing on them). B Company continued to provide security for fire support base Veghel. 2d and 3d platoons conducted reduction in force operations in the vicinity of fire support base Veghel. C Company conducted reduction in force operations from YD532088 to YD524095. D Company conducted reduction in force operations near YD502094, found four 2-man hooches and remains of fires. D-1/501 continued to provide security for fire support base Bastogne.

February 2nd - Battalion continued reduction in force operations at YD498091. 3d platoon, D Company found an old 3-4 man sleeping area, 1 pair rubber sandals, 1 fishnet, and cooking utensils. D-1/501 continued to provide security for fire support base Bastogne and mine sweep to fire support base Birmingham.

February 3rd - A Company moved to fire support base Bastogne and assumed security of Bastogne. D Company and Recon platoon moved to land zone Sally. D-1/501 was released from operational control 1/502.

February 4th - No change from previous day.

February 5th - D Company moved from landing zone Sally to fire support base T-Bone. A-1/501 became operational control 1/502d. A Company conducted reduction in force from T-Bone to YD642187. At 1420 hours in vicinity YD644191 the point man was attacked by a tiger. There were negative US casualties, and the tiger was wounded.

February 6th - C Company conducted a reduction in force to fire support base Bastogne and then moved by truck to Sally. The rest of the battalion continued its security missions and conducted reduction in force operations and saturation patrols.

February 7th - The battalion continued securing fire support base Bastogne, Veghel and T-Bone. A-1/501 conducted reduction in force operations to landing zone Sally and was released operational control.

February 8th - B Company moved from fire support base Veghel to landing zone Sally. Battalion headquarters and tactical operation center command post conducted a move from fire support base Veghel to Omaha and Sally.

February 9th - A Company moved from fire support base Bastogne to Sally. Companies C and D and Recon platoon conducted saturation patrols. Operation SHERMAN PEAK ended. The battalion continued to participate in Operation NEVADA EAGLE.

February 10th - B Company moved from landing zone Sally to YD-62401 and conducted a reduction in force at YD626172 where the company found 72 old bunkers. C Company moved to Sally and then conducted a combat assault to 4 ambush positions. D Company was established at fire support base T-Bone. At 2040 in vicinity YD658219 3d platoon sprung an ambush on Viet Cong moving along a trail from west to east. The Viet Cong were engaged with claymores and small arms. There were negative results. Recon platoon moved to landing zone Sally.

February 11th - A Company conducted a combat assault from landing zone Sally to YD589155 and then conducted reduction in force operation. B Company conducted saturation patrols and established ambush positions. At YD631167 1st platoon found 6 new bunkers, 70 pounds fresh rice, 700 AK47 rounds, 2 hooches and some tools. Company conducted saturation patrols in vicinity YD6929. D Company continued to provide security for fire support base T-Bone.

331

Recon platoon conducted a combat assault from landing zone Sally to YD589155 and conducted a reduction in force operation.

February 12th - The battalion continued with patrols and ambushes. At 1635 at YD582154 Recon platoon initiated contact on an estimated 10 North Vietnamese Army moving on a trail. The action resulted in 1 US wounded in action, 1 North Vietnamese Army killed in action, 1 AK47, 4 rucksacks, 1 radio and 1 surgical kit captured.

February 13th - The battalion continued with patrols and ambushes. at 1100 at YD628166 B Company, 1st platoon made contact with an enemy force. The results were 5 US wounded in action and 1 US killed in action. There was negative assessment of enemy casualties. At 0930 at YD578154 Recon platoon made contact resulting in 1 US wounded.

MENDEZ JOHN WILLIAM   SGT 20 13-Feb-69 B CO
MORRIS BEDFORD MARK JR   SP4 23 13-Feb-69 B CO

February 14th - A Company received fire from an unknown element resulting in 1 US wounded in action. C Company moved to fire support base T-Bone and assumed the security at T-Bone. D Company moved off of fire support base T-Bone and conducted patrols and established ambushes.

February 15th - Today A Company, 2d platoon engaged 2 Viet Cong at YD578148 resulting in 1 US wounded in action, 1 Viet Cong killed in action and 1 AK47 captured. B Company, 2d platoon at YD628165 engaged 2 North Vietnamese Army resulting in 1 North Vietnamese Army killed in action, 1 North Vietnamese Army wounded in action, 1 AK47 and 1 rocket propelled grenade launcher captured. There were negative US casualties. The rest of the battalion continued conducting patrols and establishing ambushes, with C Company providing security on fire support base T-Bone.

February 16th - The battalion continued to conduct patrols and ambushes. AT YD624166 B Company, 2d platoon engaged 1 North Vietnamese Army with small arms resulting in 1 North Vietnamese Army killed in action and 1 SKS captured. Later in the day the 2d platoon engaged another North Vietnamese Army at the same location resulting in 1 North Vietnamese Army killed in action and 1 AK47 captured. AT YD694306 D Company, 2d platoon engaged 3 sampans and sunk one of them.

February 17th - The battalion assumed a primarily defensive posture as today was the start of the Tet ceasefire. The only activity was the sending out of security patrols.

February 18th - The battalion carried out patrols and ambushes. In the vicinity of YD6316 Recon platoon found several bunkers that were recently used, a bunker complex, and several burned out hooches.

February 19th - The battalion continued to conduct reduction in force operations and established ambushes. The radar at fire support base T-Bone reported movement of 2-3 persons in vicinity YD648209. 81mm mortars fired but a first light check showed negative results.

February 20th - At YD579147 A Company, 3d platoon spotted 1 Viet Cong on a trail. He was killed by a Viet Cong hand grenade booby trap resulting 1 Viet Cong killed in action and 1 AK47 captured. The rest of the battalion conducted reduction in force operations and ambushes with C Compnay continuing to provide security for fire support base T-Bone.

February 21st - The only contact made today was by B Company 1st platoon at YD624206. They engaged 6 Viet Cong with small arms. Results were 1 Viet Cong killed in action and 1 AK47 captured.

February 22nd - There was no contact made today. The battalion continued with its normal operations. D Company moved to landing zone Sally and then moved via CH47.   B Company, 1st platoon found a diary belonging to the Viet Cong killed yesterday. The diary contained much information about trails in the area.

February 23rd - A Company moved to fire support base T-Bone and assumed the responsibility of providing security for T-Bone. C Company moved from fire support base T-Bone to landing zone Sally. Recon platoon also moved to landing zone Sally, 2d Battalion intelligence reported on this day, that the North Vietnamese Army and Viet Cong plan to launch attacks on major cities and military installations on February 22nd and 23rd.

February 24th - A Continued to provide security at fire support base T-Bone. B Company conducted a reduction in force operation to Omaha and set out ambushes. D Company sent out patrols and ambushes also. C Company and Recon platoon remained at landing zone Sally.

February 25th - Companies B and C were operational control 1/501. Recon platoon moved from Sally to Omaha and conducted a reduction in force operation with 1 platoon of Popular Forces. A Company remained at fire support base T-Bone and company D conducted a reduction in force.
JOHNSON PHIL DAVID   1LT 26 25-Feb-69 C CO
WALSH TRUMAN   SP4 20 25-Feb-69 C CO

February 26th and 27th - The battalion conducted normal operations with negative results. B and C Companies remained operational control to 1/501.

February 28th - C Company was released operational control 1/501 and returned to landing zone Sally. At YD595174 D Company, 2d platoon found 4 hooches, 1 60mm mortar, various tools, and some ammunition. Recon platoon continued to operate with a platoon of Popular Forces. Operation NEVADA EAGLE ended.

About the Authors

Tom and Daisy are a father daughter team who have collaborated to bring his Vietnam story to life.

Tom lives in Glide, Oregon with his wife where he is surrounded by family and animals on their ranch. He is a devoted husband, father and grandfather. He is involved with the VFW and is now the Post Chaplain.

Daisy lives in Medford, Oregon with her husband and two kids where she is a sales assistant. She is involved in her church and keeps busy being a soccer and dance mom.

Contact Tom and Daisy at
SITPOHH@gmail.com
Facebook: T North D Willard
Instagram: safeintheperimeterofhishands
Twitter: @InPerimeter

Made in the USA
Monee, IL
08 June 2022